T0208833

The Danger of Celebrity in Power:
The Case of Liberia

JOSIAH FLOMO JOEKAI, JR.

authorHOUSE®

AuthorHouse™
1663 Liberty Drive
Bloomington, IN 47403
www.authorhouse.com
Phone: 1 (800) 839-8640

author photo credits: Amos Kaffehz

Published by AuthorHouse 04/11/2019

ISBN: 978-1-7283-0151-8 (sc)
ISBN: 978-1-7283-0150-1 (hc)
ISBN: 978-1-7283-0152-5 (e)

Library of Congress Control Number: 2019902071

Print information available on the last page.

Contents

Reflection

The Danger of Celebrity in Power: The Case of Liberia takes you on an engaging journey that dissects the rise of celebrities to political power and unravels the implications of their imposing rule, sometimes to the detriment of democracy's growth and development.

In particular, the book delves into the small West African nation of Liberia as an embryonic and fragile democracy with many years of social, economic, and political decadence. There, to the shock of the world, a footballer, George Oppong Manneh Weah, was elected president in 2017.

My intent is not to cast doom but to realistically unearth the dangerous effects that are rapidly emerging in Liberia since the footballer assumed power. The visible indicators of what is to come are extensively discussed in this book.

It is absolutely prudent to underscore that mediocrity has taken over Liberia with the election of a football star, whose entire background is completely unrelated to the functions of the presidency. President Weah has no credible corporate or political leadership experience; thus he lacks the background and savoir-faire to lead Liberia out of its current fragility and degradation onto a trajectory of sustainable peace and stability.

In less than twelve months into his leadership, the president has grossly and repeatedly violated the laws of Liberia, demonstrated intolerance toward the opposition, and continuously threatened advocates (i.e., critical voices), portending the emergence of tyranny.

President Weah has called the opposition "enemies of the state"; said to the Liberian people, "I cannot fight corruption because everyone is related"; and said to the BBC stringer in Liberia, Jonathan Paye-Layleh, "You were one of those against me when I was advocating for peace." Certainly, these statements are worrisome; coming from the heart of a rookie president, overwhelmingly elected with 61.5 percent of the total valid votes cast, in less than twelve months. The implications of such tyrannical moves are enormous and must not be discounted. Obviously, these are scary times, which reflect a looming danger. The trend cannot continue unabated.

About the Author

The author is a Liberian writer and development practitioner with expertise in elections, education, and security administration. He is an inspirational speaker and a social justice advocate. In 2015, he received an award for Outstanding Service as a Presenter during the Great Gathering of the African Descent Lutherans in the Americas (ADLA) and Association of Liberian Lutherans in the Americas (ALLIA) in Baltimore, Maryland, in the United States. The author is married and blessed with three boys.

Acknowledgment

I am exceptionally grateful for the strong support of my family: my wife, Joana, and the boys: Joe-Joe, Zick, and Josiah.

Dedication

This book is dedicated to all those who strive for the betterment of society by seeking to create a democratic space with the tenets of fair play, equality, and justice.

In particular, this book is dedicated to the already wearied but resilient Liberians in hopes that it will arouse sober reflection and engender a genuine sense of renewal in their collective search for decent and productive leadership for Liberia .

Prologue

Indisputably, Liberia is the oldest independent African nation, but the country has a peculiar and interesting history. Born out of slavery in the 1800s, Liberia's journey from its establishment in 1822 through independence in 1847 and then to the twenty-first century is replete with tales of extreme poverty, illiteracy, and gross underdevelopment fueled by more than a century and a half of inequality, exclusion, and pervasive corruption.

The prolonged leadership dominance of the so-called ruling elites (freed slaves and their descendants) to the disadvantage of the locals (native Africans) obviously inaugurated a deeply rooted divide in the body politic of Liberia. Two long-standing inclinations seem to persist: the so-called Americo-Liberian hegemony and the indigenous heritage claim. This divide is a major factor that accounts for the years of political, social, and economic instability in Liberia. The failure by successive governments to bridge this long-standing gap has culminated in the undeserving state of the nation. So the establishment of Liberia on such a divisive platform and the many years of dominant and insensitive reign of the America-Liberian hegemony gave rise to acrimony, violent conflicts, and the eventual breakdown of the country up to 2003.

So it is unfortunate that in spite of being independent since the 1800s, Liberia is still struggling to come up to speed with many of its contemporaries in the twenty-first century. The country is one of the least developed in the world. Liberia's history of violence and instability has left serious scars on its already fragile economy. In 2013, Liberia was ranked fourth poorest worldwide, with a GDP per capita of $710, by the International Monetary Fund. With some progress toward democratic enhancement from 2005 following the civil war, the country's GDP experienced a slight rise to 2017 with a GDP per capita of $860.83. However, this doesn't show any significant growth as reflected by the present appalling economy.

The year 2017 provided a golden opportunity for Liberians to choose to elect a leader who would consolidate the democratic gains made over the past twelve years (2005–2017) and surmount the challenges of reviving the economy for sustainable recovery and development. The election was expected to record the second smooth leadership transition in the country in seventy years. Madam Ellen Johnson Sirleaf, the sitting president, was expected to turn over power to an elected president. The last time it happened was in 1944, when President Edwin Barclay turned over power to President William V. S. Tubman.

The 2017 election was crucial to Liberia's transformation. It drew the attention of the world, particularly as it would be a transition from an African woman's leadership. After the second female president in Africa, Madam Joyce Binda of Malawi, failed to succeed herself as a result of her government's being embroiled in corruption, Madam Sirleaf was under the spotlight. The reason was simple. A smooth transition meant a lot for the maturity of Liberia's democracy as well as women's leadership in Africa and, by extension, the world.

All this began to play out in sharp contrast to the ideals of democracy. Madam Sirleaf had a plan. Her plan was manifestly not in the country's interest: it was meant to inaugurate a president of her choosing, enabling her to retain her grip on power in her post presidential life. To the utter dismay of the world, a football icon, George Oppong Manneh Weah, who had opposed her twice in the 2005 and 2011 elections was elected with the help of President Sirleaf over an outstanding statesman and administrator, Ambassador Joseph Nyuma Boakai, former vice president of Liberia.

A great deal went wrong during the elections. The entire process was characterized by maneuverings and manipulations, with many fingers pointed at President Sirleaf and the authorities of the National Elections Commission (NEC). Strangely, the president, who is a Nobel laureate and first female president in Africa, was accused by her own party, the Unity Party (UP), and by pundits of supporting the candidate of the opposition Congress for Democratic Change, Mr. Weah.

True to her own word, Madam Sirleaf did not lend support in any measure to her own vice president, the standard-bearer of the Unity Party, Ambassador Boakai, who served her for the twelve years of her presidency with diligence, loyalty, and dedication.

Madam Sirleaf fell out with the party that made her president in 2005 and stood firm in getting her reelected in 2011, abandoning at the same time the presidential bid of Ambassador Boakai. The paradox is that the former president and her vice president had neither a political relationship nor one of convenience at the time. They enjoyed a longstanding relationship ever since their secondary school days at the College of West Africa in Monrovia. The two looked out for each other as genuine friends or siblings would do. They became great companions and got their families to know each other.

Naturally, selecting Ambassador Boakai to serve as her running mate was a decision not of political convenience but firmly anchored on trust and confidence. The twelve years of outstanding leadership support he gave to Madam

Sirleaf in her presidency reflected his commitment to the years of true friendship and distinguished service to country. In essence, Madam Sirleaf repaid Ambassador Boakai with betrayal by sacrificing many decades of a rewarding friendship for her selfish political interest.

Apart from her own party's falling out with her, there were instances in which the president acted in a way to demonstrate her support for the CDC standard-bearer, Ambassador Weah. Many of her government officials and confidants, some of whom were also officials and members of her party, defected to support the CDC candidate.

The president's silence demonstrated her consent especially in the midst of wide allegations of financial support from such individuals to candidate Weah's campaign. Prominent among government officials and partisans of the Unity Party who defected were Madam Sirleaf's minister of finance, Amara M. Konneh; her president pro tempore of the Liberian Senate, Gbehzohngar N. Finley; her minister of information, cultural affairs, and tourism and secretary general of the UP, Len Eugene Nagbe; and her son, Robert Sirleaf. In the caravan to the CDC also were junior party officials and cronies of the former president.

Another dimension of Madam Sirleaf's duplicity was her many public appearances with the opposition CDC standard-bearer, Weah, at public events like launches, dedications, and groundbreaking ceremonies during the campaign period. Former President Sirleaf shocked Liberians and the world with her conspicuous campaign boost to candidate Weah.

A particular event that generated much attention was the symbolic start of the highly anticipated Gbarnga-Menekoma road project. When completed, the paved corridor stretching from Gbarnga, central Liberia, through Liberia's breadbasket, Lofa County, to neighboring Sierra Leone. The envisaged superhighway will connect Liberia to Sierra Leone and Guinea with ease. Thus, it will certainly have great economic and development significance.

Exploiting this opportunity, Madam Sirleaf organized the official launch of the project and invited candidate Weah and his running mate, Senator Jewel Howard-Taylor, but did not invite Ambassador Boakai. The launch ritual was performed by the former president, candidate Weah, and Howard-Taylor, visibly confirming Madam Sirleaf's support for a Weah presidency. Her goal was to attract votes from both vote-rich Lofa and Bong Counties and, by extension, the entire north-central region of the country for the Weah–Howard-Taylor ticket.

This situation stimulated the serious accusation that the president had undermined her vice president's campaign, but she denied knowing about the attendance of the opposition candidates, even though she recognized and formally shared the platform with them. Interestingly, a few weeks later, candidate Weah in an interview confirmed that he had been invited to the ceremony by the former president, and he was grateful to her for the invitation and her support. The interview video went viral as Madam Sirleaf's integrity continued to erode.

Candidate Weah was by all accounts the direct beneficiary of the state machinery. Madam Sirleaf provided the CDC candidate with funding to finance the West African Examinations Council (WEAC) fees for secondary school students. WEAC fees were always borne by parents and students as their part of the cost of education. It is not a policy of the government to pay WEAC fees for students. However, as part of the former president's scheme to see candidate Weah elected, her government claimed that it was unable to pay its share of WEAC fees to qualify 2017 candidates for public exams. This strange turn of events was introduced at the height of the hard-fought campaign. Although the action of the former president was condemned, her plans worked out the way she had planned. It was a way to secure the votes of eligible secondary school students for candidate Weah. Soon candidate Weah announced that he was paying the fees for all candidates to the public exams. In a society ridden by poverty where parents and students lack the means to raise the fees, Madam Sirleaf's strategy worked.

On a daily basis, secondary school students trooped to the headquarters of the CDC to receive their fees. For the entire campaign period, students from across Montserrado County and counties adjacent like Grand Bassa, Margibi, and Bomi were found on commercial vehicles and motorcycles and along major streets, dressed in full uniforms, headed directly to candidate Weah. That was one of the strategies that President Sirleaf deceptively deployed to turn a mediocre candidate, Weah, into a virtual messiah. The uninformed young voters were induced to believe that the footballer was the antidote to Liberia's chronic underdevelopment and economic disaster President Sirleaf helped create.

Because every gesture deserves appreciation, Weah expressed appropriate gratitude to the president for providing the funds to cover students' WEAC fees, admitting that this was a clear manifestation of President Sirleaf's support to his candidacy. The president's favorite candidate, footballer Weah had no idea of the pitfalls of exposing his benefactor by openly expressing gratitude for her support to his campaign. Truly, it would have become a real danger were the actions of President Sirleaf not well concocted. The silence of the National Elections Commission, without any inquiry into possible campaign finance violations or vote buying, spoke to the extent of the outgoing president's interference in the 2017 elections.

President Sirleaf's efforts to influence the 2017 elections were not only noticed domestically. The ECOWAS region and Africa as a whole got very concerned about the disturbing news of President Sirleaf's engagement in acts that would tend to undermine the sanctity of the elections and by extension the democratic gains the country had made in the last decade. The chair of the Authority of Heads of State of the African Union (AU), Guinean President Professor Alpha Conde; and the chair of Heads of Authority of ECOWAS, Togolese President Faure Gnassingbe, paid an urgent courtesy visit to Monrovia and had a meeting with President Sirleaf. In that meeting, Alpha Conde did not mince words. He cautioned Madam Sirleaf to stay above the fray. President Conde's caution was an embarrassment to Madam Sirleaf who had been deemed an advocate of social justice and democracy for many years. As a test of women's leadership in Africa, it was demeaning for the president of a country like Guinea, which was struggling to fully subscribe to the tenets of democracy, to caution Madam Sirleaf, a Nobel laureate, on her handling of a crucial leadership transition. It was baffling, but the reality was obvious. Madam Sirleaf's role in manipulating the 2017 election was visible.

The electoral process itself suffered several mishaps, some of which were well orchestrated by the National Elections Commission (NEC), from the registration of voters to the polling on election day. The registration data of thousands of voters were either omitted or duplicated. The Elections Commission itself admitted to the Liberian Senate and its various news conferences the improprieties through its chairman, Jerome G. Korkoya.

The omission and duplication of voters' names and other detailed information led to two fundamental wrongs. First, those whose data was not found in the voter roll were affected in two ways. Some were allowed to vote with their information recorded on a separate sheet of paper, referred to as addendum; others were prevented from voting due to the omission of their data. Those whose information was duplicated had the opportunity of voting several times. Many voters, especially young voters, were seen roaming from one center to another on election day, doing everything possible to vote two or more times. This situation was reported by journalists, independent observers, monitors, and political party representatives. The situation became so serious that the Elections Commission had to engage in a robust media campaign to assure the public that they were addressing the situation. As a result, even with their voter identification cards, many voters were unable to vote, thus losing the opportunity to exercise their franchise.

Another piece of election irregularity was the chaotic voter registration exercise. The credibility of any election begins with the integrity of the voter roll, because it is the roll that determines the number and eligibility of voters. Without a voter roll, you cannot have credible elections. In the event, however, if such an election is deemed not credible, it often proceeds anyhow without a credible roll.

The irregularity and fraud questions that beset the 2017 elections generated serious apprehensions about the credibility of the elections. Many feared that the NEC lacked the credibility to deliver the elections in a free, fair, and credible manner. To the dismay of the public, former President Sirleaf and the opposition CDC persistently spoke out in defense of NEC, expressing absolute confidence in the electoral management body despite the constant public outcry and international concerns about the credibility of the elections.

Second, polling on October 10, 2017, also recorded several incidents that amounted to fraud and irregularities. The NEC created a special online data system that accounted for certain voters' particulars that were omitted from the Final Registration Roll (FRR) without the knowledge and consent of participating political parties. Registered voters in that category were made to vote and record their names separately. Only the NEC knew how the online data system worked and how such data would feed into the FRR. This mechanism created a floodgate for illegal voting, as many voters cast their ballots without being accounted for by the FRR.

The magnitude of the situation caused the Liberty Party of Counselor Charles Walker Brumskine to challenge the October 10, 2017, result, describing it as an election characterized by fraud and irregularities and calling for a rerun of the election. The Unity Party of Ambassador Joseph Nyuma Boakai joined the Liberty Party as cocomplainant in the election fraud and irregularities case, which was originally filed with the office of the Hearing Officer in keeping with the elections complaints management framework of the Elections Commission.

The NEC, as the electoral management body of Liberia, has quasi-judicial powers, which gives it the right to hear elections-related cases involving either fraud or irregularity. However, any party to such a contest that takes exception to the ruling of the Hearing Office of the NEC has the right to appeal to the NEC Board of Commissioners. Similarly, if the opinion or ruling of the board is not acceptable to any of the parties involved, the party may take an appeal to the Supreme Court of Liberia. The Supreme Court, as the final arbiter of justice, reviews the case, hears the final arguments, and renders the final judgment.

The case was heard by the hearing office of the NEC; hearing officer Attorney Muana Ville ruled in favor of the NEC. In his ruling, the attorney denied the Liberty Party and the Unity Party petition for rerun of the October 10, 2017, elections on grounds of fraud and irregularities. He justified his ruling by asserting that although the NEC encountered some problems, those problems were identified and corrected. Therefore, they did not constitute fraud and irregularities such as to warrant a rerun of the elections. The two parties immediately took an appeal to the Board of Commissioners of the NEC. After a review of the case file, the board upheld the decision of its hearing officer. The Liberty Party responded by appealing to the Supreme Court of Liberia.

Obviously, seeking legal recourse is an acceptable democratic norm. That in fact makes justice a nonnegotiable element of democracy; legal recourse is practiced in every democratic system. However, the action of the Liberty Party along with the Unity Party to take this matter before the full bench of the Court was detested by President Ellen Johnson Sirleaf and her newly found ally, the opposition CDC. Unfortunately, the president, who was a beneficiary of Liberia's hard-earned democracy for two consecutive terms (twelve years), described the actions of the Liberty Party and Unity Party as an assault on Liberia's democracy.

Absolutely, the case involving the Liberty Party and the NEC was so critical and sensitive that it delayed the runoff election between the CDC of Ambassador George Oppong Manneh Weah and the Unity Party of Ambassador Boakai. However, the actions of the two parties were the best approach by democratic standards to deal with such a crucial electoral matter rather than resorting to any move that would trigger violence. The president's comments about an assault on Liberia's democracy were sturdily condemned and rejected. From all indications, President Sirleaf was determined to deliver the election to Candidate Weah, no matter what. The deep division caused by President Sirleaf's role created uncertainty for a smooth transition, as the country was experiencing heightened political tension. Citizens were consumed by fear of violence, and the already weakening economy became stagnant.

The Supreme Court was in the spotlight. The country's future depended on the high court's decision. Liberians were visibly divided along party lines, and of course, Madam Sirleaf and cohorts were lined up behind the CDC and the NEC. There were two public opinions. One averred that a rerun was imminent, given the litany of evidence, while the other insisted that the court would dismiss rerun. The court was under pressure and understood the magnitude of the decision it had to make.

Liberians were eager and very impatient. Media institutions were set to capture every aspect of the ruling. Political parties were nervous. Then on December 7, 2017, the Supreme Court finally issued its ruling.

> The Honorable Supreme Court has defined
> fraud as the employment of trick, artifice or

deception to cheat or mislead another and it is not sufficient to merely allege fraud as a basis for relief, it must be established by proof.

Accordingly, we hold that the Hearing Officer did not err, and the first and second appellant for a rerun of the October 10 2017 elections is hereby denied.

Wherefore and in view of the foregoing, appellants' appeal is hereby denied.

Thus, the court denied the Liberty Party's appeal for a rerun and ordered the NEC to proceed to conduct a runoff election in accordance with the constitution, elections law, and the rules set forth in the ruling.

That was the decision of the court of arbitration. No matter one's disposition, the ruling would not change. Still, many felt that the decision (4–1) of the court was partial and very unfair.

Justice Kabineh Ja'neh handed down an elaborate dissenting opinion, in which he differed with his colleagues, emphasizing that irregularities had occurred. No matter their degree, the matter should be considered a violation of the law. Therefore, the appellant should not be denied her appeal. Although Ja'neh's opinion was important, clearly addressing the dictates of the law, it had no effect on the ruling of the majority. So the runoff election had to go ahead between the two parties that had obtained the highest numbers of votes. According to the NEC, the CDC had received 38.4 percent, and the UP received 28.8 percent.

The management of the election was just one aspect of Liberia's democratic transition. Although it was important, another crucial aspect was the need for Liberians to elect a president with the know-how to undertake the herculean task of strengthening and improving the country's fragile democracy, reviving its broken economy, and navigating its international challenges.

Based on the enormity of the problems confronting Liberia, it was inconceivable that Liberians would clamor to elect a soccer icon, George Oppong Manneh Weah, over his opponent, Ambassador Joseph N. Boakai, an outstanding statesman with many years of leadership experience. The former vice president is a committed and dedicated public servant with many years of service in both public and private sectors. He is a distinguished diplomat, agriculturalist, educationalist, and outstanding administrator.

Weah has an unmatched legacy in soccer on the African continent and the world as a whole. His accomplishments in the soccer world also put Liberia on the soccer map and created an exposure for many young people who succeeded in developing their potential in the field. He remains an inspiration to his generation and those to come.

Notwithstanding these achievements in soccer, Weah is simply a celebrity with an extravagant lifestyle. He has a short attention span and is a showman with a huge appetite for pageantry. Clearly, Weah has little or no credible corporate or political leadership experience. As such, he's not capable of leading Liberia out of the present economic paralysis and putting it on the trajectory of social, political, and economic stability. His election at this critical period of Liberia's transformation has implications for country's recovery and development drive.

Besides the uncertainty about President Weah's competence, his election as the first celebrity president of Liberia and the African continent has brought a paradigm shift on both Liberian and African politics in general. By all accounts, Weah's election, like that of the reality TV star Donald Trump, now president of the United States of America, has the potential to inspire a momentous shift to politics by celebrities in Africa. If caution is not taken, this phenomenon will impede the progress of democracy in Africa.

Undeniably, the election of Mr. Weah has created serious doubts in the minds of many Liberians about the survival of democracy. They are deeply concerned about the state of the rule of law, freedom of speech, freedom of the press, protection of human rights, and the alleviation of poverty under a leader they believe has no idea about the job with which he has been entrusted.

Chapter 1

A Closer Look at a Nation in Transition

The founding of Liberia can be directly traced to the United States' domestic politics on slave trade as well as its foreign policy interests in the 1800s. Such policy interests arose in the aftermath of the abolition of the transatlantic slave trade. So many slaves had gained their freedom by then that apprehension spread that the freed people would be acculturated to the normal American lifestyle, something they were denied during the entire period of their enslavement. The growing number of freed slaves generated much concern and became a topical issue discussed with interest across every segment of American society.

The magnitude of the future implications of the presence of freed slaves led to consideration of the domestic and foreign policy questions. From the religious standpoint, moral and justice questions emerged. Abolitionists were concerned about the possibility of the creation of African

American society, and policymakers thought they would explore the use of former slaves to expand and improve the labor force and the military, thus strengthening the economy and security of the United States. In essence, the transition from slaves to free people of color ushered in a crucial epoch in American history while at the same time giving birth to Africa's oldest republic.

The debate on what to do with the increasing number of freed slaves in the United States took a turn in 1816, when a completely white group of Americans formed the American Colonization Society (ACS) as a medium to address the problem. The ACS's goal was to resettle freed slaves in Africa.

The ACS project gained momentum when it gained the support of certain prominent Americans. The ACS claimed that the freed slaves were capable of governing themselves and spreading Christianity to Africa, emphasizing that slavery was morally wrong and constituted the practice of injustice. Whether or not the ACS was realistic about their claim, in truth slavery was indeed morally wrong and amounted to a serious crime against humanity. So for many, the move by the ACS to resettle freed black slaves in Africa was appropriate.

In no time, several well-known Americans joined the movement, the ACS in its resettlement drive. Prominent among them were Henry Clay, Daniel Webster, and

John Randolph. The ACS movement gained momentum when former President Thomas Jefferson made a public declaration of support to the organization, followed by President James Madison. President Madison went all out and succeeded in mobilizing public resources to support the goals of the ACS. An initial amount of one hundred thousand dollars was raised in support of the ACS mission.

In spite of this popular movement which received the blessings of succeeding US governments, its vision was strongly resisted by several abolitionists, both black and white, on the basis that it was impossible for races to integrate. In particular, they did not like the idea of establishing an African American colony in Africa and deceptively averred that it was not possible.

The ideological difference with the ACS did not really make a major difference because the ACS had already gained the recognition and support it needed to proceed with its mission of resettling freed slaves in Africa. The members of the ACS were enthusiastic and made plans to embark on the journey. The political will was favorable, and the resources were coming as expected. In essence, the stage was set.

In 1821, the first target for the settlers was Sherbro Island off the coast of West Africa. While at Sherbro, many of the settlers got sick and died from malaria. So they were moved to Providence Island, further south along the coast, where living conditions for them were said to be much better; thus they settled there.

Relations between the settlers and local leaders were not rosy. They were understandably resisted by local leaders when they attempted to purchase land to expand their settlement. Such resistance arose from differences in culture and orientation. Besides, the settlers took a superior posture, striking indigenous people as redolent of arrogance and dominance. With deep insensitivity to the existence and authority of the indigenous, they proceeded in an overbearing manner, treating the indigenous with disdain. However, following intermittent conflicts, the navy officer in charge by then, Robert Stockton, persuaded the local leaders and succeeded in securing the sought land.

The group of settlers at Sherbro were moved to the new location, and a chain of settlements were created along the west coast. In 1822, several other freed slaves joined the group at the new location called Providence Island. The acquisition of the land and subsequent settlement did not however end conflict between the settlers and the indigenous. Attacks on the settlers by local tribes persisted, leading the settlers to raise fortifications for their own protection. In spite of the persistent conflict influenced by the settlers/indigenous cultural divide, the population of all the settlements combined rapidly grew to about twenty thousand by 1824. The settlement was immediately named

Liberia, with its capital dubbed Monrovia in honor of US President James Monroe. Understandably, President Monroe provided more funding to the ACS project. So naming Monrovia after him was a way of honoring him for his support to the settlement process.

The abolition of the transatlantic slave trade witnessed the influx of freed slaves on the shores of Africa, the West Coast in particular. The US Navy persistently removed slaves from ships loaded with slaves along the coast and put them ashore in Liberia, to the advantage of those slaves and disadvantage of their masters. This action was in keeping with the US policy commitment to the abolition of the slave trade and the resettlement of freed slaves in Africa.

The first phase of the ACS mission was well on course with continuing settlement in Liberia. The United States adopted a new policy toward the settlers: to provide them money to engage in commerce in order to become self-sufficient. The idea was for the settlers to become independent with stronger reliance on commerce.

However, a huge presence of British and French traders continuously encroached on Liberia's territory. The colony struggled to defend its territory, which defined the scope of commerce by then. Unfortunately, Liberia was not a sovereign state. So it continued to lose territory to the British and French, who had well-organized and stronger colonies. The United States did not do much to discourage the aggression of the British and French, so Liberia was steadily losing both territory and commercial strength. Even in the face of moderate diplomatic assistance to the Liberian colony by the United States in the face of the aggression, the British and French were in better positions to extend their territorial expansions.

As a direct result of these territorial advances, Liberia had no option but to declare independence from the ACS in 1847 in order to become sovereign and create its own laws mainly on commerce. Thus on July 26, 1847, Liberia joined Haiti as the first two black nations of the world.

Liberia's declaration of independence was not favorably received in the United States. In particular, Washington did not extend diplomatic recognition to the new republic, a nation that it had in effect created. This action was on account of the impact that Liberia's independence could have on slavery in the United States. The irony was that unlike the British, French, and Portuguese, the United States did not get directly involved with the establishment of Liberia. Instead, it used the ACS as a proxy organization to act on its behalf. Still, the American republic had a vested interest contrary to the ACS's goal of resettling freed slaves in Africa.

The ACS was established on the moral principle that slavery was wrong, and so its idea as a movement against the slave trade was welcomed by many. In spite of both huge support to the ACS project and the apprehension among the citizenry and some abolitionists about the spontaneously growing number of freed slaves in the American society, the US government sought to retain the freed slaves mainly for economic and security reasons—particularly to strengthen the labor force and build a stronger military. That is why following Liberia's independence from the ACS, the influx of freed slaves into Liberia was halted on the basis of this policy. The number fell dramatically.

As the situation unfolded, the United States could not even recognize or do business with Liberia for fifteen years, until 1862, when at last the decision was made to establish diplomatic relations with Liberia. By contrast, despite protests against Liberia's independence by the affected British companies, London was the first to extend recognition to the new republic, signing a treaty of commerce and friendship with Monrovia in 1848.

Ever since independence in 1847, Liberia has been haunted by a legacy of bad governance reflective of poverty, disease, and illiteracy. This has resulted from systemic inequality and exclusion that held sway from the days of the first settlement of freed slaves in Liberia in 1822 to the bloody coup d'état of 1980 and the outbreak of the brutal armed conflict in 1989.

The prevailing political culture proved incapable of producing genuine leadership able to address the dilemmas of the policies of the American Colonization Society (ACS), native Liberian independence claims, and Americo-Liberian hegemony. Thus, Africa's first republic developed an institutionalized system of autocratic governance, which succeeded itself for more than one hundred years, thereby alienating majority of the citizens in their own country. This visible divide remains unresolved and continues to fuel the odium and acrimony in our body politic.

Thus, despite abundant and enviable natural resources such as diamonds, gold, iron ore, vast rainforest, and rubber, the country could not develop in the absence of good governance backed by the rule of law.

Liberia's independence history is indeed a bizarre journey. After 171 years of existence as a so-called sovereign nation, the country is still an object of extremely poor and suffering people and least among equals. Sadly, Liberians have a long history of being victims of their own choices at the polls. Although the "so say one, so say all" dictatorial era of President William V. S. Tubman ended after his death in 1971, it was a major suppressive factor during his regime.

Following his demise, his successor, President William R. Tolbert Jr., embarked on his "from mat to mattress" policy, poised to engender social, political, and economic integration. President Tolbert demonstrated genuine commitment evidenced by his pro-poor economic policy to revive the economy and promote integration and unity among citizens. President Tolbert began to invest significantly in secondary education to improve its quality and make it a foundation for opportunities to young Liberians to study abroad in the sciences, governance, and agriculture. He also attracted tremendous support to the agriculture sector which witnessed expansion and job creation. The World Bank's agriculture development projects in Bong, Lofa, and Nimba created many jobs for Liberians and gave the economy a boost. President Tolbert was viewed by many as the unifier who would have appropriately bridged the longstanding Americo-Liberian/indigenous divide.

Unfortunately, the president was a victim of heightened political tensions in the country, culminating in the infamous rice riot in 1979 amid dissatisfaction over the increasing price of rice, the country's staple food. The rice riot led to chaos in Monrovia causing deaths and destruction of property. Additionally, the president's non-alliance policy, which he used to expand the country's relations and attract support for his pro-poor policy, also caused international stir and concern, especially at the height of the Cold War.

In 1980, President Tolbert was murdered in a bloody coup d'état. Thirteen of his cabinet ministers were also killed by a firing squad on the orders of the leader of the People's Redemption Council (PRC), Master Sergeant Samuel K. Doe. Embracing the military junta, Liberians took to the streets across the country, ignorantly singing to the glorification of the bloody coup makers "native woman born soldier, soldier killed Tolbert." This gruesome act committed by the military junta opened an awful chapter in the country's political history with serious consequences for governance in the years ahead.

Mr. Doe and his PRC ruled the country on decrees for a period of five years from 1980 to 1985, at which time he was strongly pressured by certain Western powers, especially the United States, to turn power over to civilian leadership through democratic elections. Mr. Doe smartly rewrote the constitution, fashioned to suit his presidential bid and anticipated rule.

The new constitution was adopted in 1986. Prior to the adoption, the president organized a kangaroo election in 1985 in which he was declared winner, intensifying political tension and acrimony in the country. His main opponents, the late Jackson F. Doe of the Liberia Action Party (LAP) and classroom teacher William Gabriel Kpolleh of the Liberian Unification Party (LUP), were subject to constant intimidation and eventually deprived of their rights and chances. In particular, Jackson F. Doe was believed to have won the 1985 elections but denied his victory by self-declared President Samuel Doe.

All these maneuverings and manipulations deprived Liberians of their choice in the 1985 elections, thereby ushering in the brutal civil war of 1989 in which President

Doe himself was gruesomely killed by Mr. Prince Y. Johnson of the then Independent National Patriotic Front of Liberia (INPFL), an offspring of Mr. Charles G. Taylor's National Patriotic Front of Liberia (NPFL).

In an effort to end the devastating civil war in 1997, a special election was organized, and former warlord Charles G. Taylor was perversely elected. With the overwhelming support he enjoyed, predominantly from thousands of his fighters spread across the country, especially young people, it was obvious for him to win. Mr. Taylor's victory in that election was also bordered on fears that should he lose, he would return to the bush with devastating consequences. Unbelievably, the popular slogan of Charles Taylor's campaign was "You kill my pa (father), you kill my ma (mother), I will vote for you." These dark times in Liberia's history speak of a misguided nation incapable of governing itself.

Notwithstanding this incredible journey, Liberia's contribution to the attainment of global peace and security cannot be dismissed. The country made immeasurable contributions in establishing regional, continental and international organizations from the 1940s and championing African freedom dating as far back as the 1950s.

Liberia was a signatory to the founding of the United Nations (UN) in 1945. Earlier, Liberia was one of the sixty-three member states that made up the League of Nations between 1920 and 1939, after which it was formally dissolved on April 18, 1946, after it transitioned into the UN. Important to note also is the fact that a Liberian, Angie Brooks Randall, once served as president of the UN General Assembly.

Under the leadership of President William V. S. Tubman, Liberia initiated the discussion leading to the formation of the Organization of African Unity (OAU), now the African Union (AU). That historic meeting took place in Saniquellie, Nimba County, July 15–19, 1959, and was hosted by President Tubman with his colleagues, Presidents Ahmed Sekou Touré of Guinea and Kwame Nkrumah of Ghana. The Saniquellie meeting was a precursor to the May 25, 1963, Addis Ababa foundational meeting of the OAU.

Liberia and Sierra Leone originally founded the Mano River Union on October 3, 1973, followed by a declaration containing five major protocols concluded by the two countries in Bo, Sierra Leone. Guinea and Côte d'Ivoire joined the MRU in 1980 and 2008, respectively. The MRU has also emerged as a great source of sub regional integration, peace, and security.

Similarly, on May 28, 1975, Liberia was a founding member of the Economic Community of West African States (ECOWAS). It is no doubt that ECOWAS contributed tremendously to ending Liberia's decade-and-a-half civil crisis. The regional body organized and deployed a peacekeeping force with troops contributed by member states. With the great leadership of ECOWAS and its standby force command, the West African peacekeeping force was able to bring the prolonged crisis to an end with support from the United Nations in 2003.

Currently, ECOWAS is supporting Liberia's recovery and development strides. In particular, ECOWAS's role in strengthening security in the aftermath of the departure of the United Nations mission in Liberia (UNMIL), the promotion of peace, trade, and regional integration remains an indelible imprint on the minds of all well-meaning Liberians.

Indisputably, Liberia's independence in 1847 inspired the independence of other African nations, especially from the 1950s, and played a pivotal role in the establishment of these historic institutions. The irony is that in spite of the leadership role Liberia has long played on the world stage, there is limited or no significant mention of such achievements in historical perspectives referencing these milestone accomplishments. Besides, Liberia's current dissipating state of domestic affairs does not reflect of these great international achievements.

Certainly, the lack of genuine leadership to unite the people and develop the country for more than a century and a half has eroded these legacies. Even with its so-called legacy-history of being the oldest independent African republic, Liberia is still struggling to come up to speed with its contemporaries in this twenty-first century. While nations are strongly competing in this era of technological advancement, Liberia is harshly confronted by poverty, disease, and illiteracy.

Chapter 2

Reflection on the Rise of Celebrity to Political Leadership

No matter the genre, celebrities (or celebs) have much in common. Celebs possess irresistible gems and acumen that give them a high public profile. With their impressive lifestyles or ways of expressing themselves, celebs impact lives by deeply appealing to people's emotion. Whether performing in sports, acting, theater, music, or the media, celebs create strong bonds that leave unfading memories.

In everyday life, people across the world never lose sight of intriguing moments in the lives of celebs. Even within their busy schedules, individuals or families take time to go to events of various types, cinemas, pageants, concerts, and theaters or watch television series, suggesting that celebs play important roles in making life worth living. Their amazing gifts and captivating utterances keep celebs firmly stuck to their audiences, no matter their field of mastery. This astounding way of life leaves imperishable imprints on people's lives and society, eventually influencing cultures and traditions.

Obviously, celebs are famous people, and they enjoy a wide range of advantages. They are adored, respected, admired, and honored, no matter the gradation. Regardless of what they do, they always have great opportunities and are given special treatment in whatever they do, how they do it, and wherever they go. Inarguably, celebs are known targets for United Nations agencies, international, and intergovernmental organizations, business, and humanitarian institutions because their fame makes them useful as goodwill ambassadors or representatives to promote the organizations' work and sell their brands.

Notwithstanding the unique characteristics of celebs and their immeasurable contributions to society, being a celebrity or famous personality has its disadvantages as well. The shared judgment is that celebrities or famous personalities have everything in life they need. Celebs are most often wealthy people. In many instances, their image can be deceptive, implying that they are superhumans with no problems and that their lives are perfect. Not all! They are humans just like ordinary people; they do get hurt, frustrated, and stressed out at times.

The paradox is that celebs always strive to keep their downside veiled for fear of diluting their nonnegotiable status. They are fully aware that the solidity of their fame depends on avoiding scandal of any kind. This is an unshakable commitment they make to themselves, and they hold on to it firmly. So although celebs often live in splendor, they do carry varying internal struggles.

Another downside is that they lack privacy to a large degree and are often criticized for their lifestyle. They make big money, amass wealth, and live in extravagance. Private life is not a choice or place for them. So the choices they make such as the clothes they wear, the foods and drinks they prefer, and the cars or aircraft they own, the places they visit, the guests they entertain, and their long-term relationships and friends all become talking points in the public domain. Hence, celebs largely do not rule their own world. Accordingly, they are soft targets of the "public COURT."

Every day the public court hands down guilty verdicts for the choices celebs make with regard to their private and public lives. Ultimately, as humans like us, celebs do have their own challenges but because of their charm, and particularly the solid bonds they have with their trusted audiences and fans, they manage to surmount those challenges.

On the very bright side, celebrities have made a positive impact on society. They have made immeasurable contributions that have transformed lives and reshaped cultures and traditions. Celebs are true agents of diversification. They cross borders, bringing together people of different races by offering a platform for tolerance, coexistence, and acceptance. Therefore, it is worth recounting some of those remarkable life-changing moments in history engendered by celebs.

Since the 1940s, persuasive revolutionary songs from great musicians became powerful tools that rallied nations to raise awareness or champion causes that alleviate human suffering and social problems. Predominantly in Europe, Africa, and the United States of America, famine, civil rights violations, wars, natural disasters, environmental abuses, and abolition were very prevalent. Thus, emancipation songs played a pivotal role in confronting injustice and inspiring social change.

Pete Seeger, a renowned civil rights activist is remembered for confronting injustice from the 1940s to the 1970s. He sang on behalf of the progressive labor movement in the 1940s and 50s, for civil rights marches and anti-Vietnam war rallies in the 1960s, and for environmental and antiwar causes in the 1970s. Pete was a mentor to many young musicians and widely known for his popular song "We Shall Overcome." Although he wasn't a frontline fighter in the spotlight like civil rights leader Martin Luther King Jr. and others, he remains notable for the powerful messages he used as weapons through songs to support the civil rights movement.

Bob Marley is one name that stands out in the musical industry globally. Between 1963 and 1981, Bob was preaching peace and love. One famous quotation—"We got to realize we are one people, or there will never be no love at all"—remains indelible. Bob's songs were enormously influential and greatly impacted the world as his lyrics moved generations to confront injustice of any magnitude. He was a consistent freedom fighter because his weapon (his music) transcended boundaries from north to south and east to west. Today, his lyrics still remain meaningful after his death at the very young age of thirty-six. His son Ziggy and wife, Rita, are upholding Bob's legacy through performing and the family charity.

Resonating still on the continent of Africa and perhaps globally is the unforgettable music of the legendary Nigerian musician, the late Sonny Okosun. In 1979 Sonny officially released his signature album *Papa's Land*. Its memorable refrain is the simple question, "Who owns Papa's land?" Okosun was a freedom fighter with a great legacy of revolutionizing Africa with his commanding songs.

Obviously, these fascinating songs got everyone constantly reciting, "We want to know / We want to know ... / Who owns Papa's Land," as he and his chorus sang. Sonny meant Africa, the land he referred to. Thus, the lyrics that follow: "Africa is my father's land / Yes, Africa is my Papa's land / Will you let my people go? We want to rule from Cape to Cairo … / Will you free my people's hands? We want to rule our papa's land." He was a great pan-Africanist.

In those days, Nigeria was fast emerging onto the global stage as a frontline nation firmly in solidarity with other African nations, particularly Angola, Mozambique, Namibia, Zimbabwe, and South Africa as they went through their serious revolutionary struggles.

So, Sonny was a real freedom fighter, using his music as a controlling weapon to decisively confront inequality and exclusion in these countries alongside other rights movements against injustice. Although one might ask how those emotive thoughts and ideas might impact today's Africa, still, Sonny's role in Africa's emancipation was profound. His lyrics strongly live in the soul of Africa.

I recall quite vividly growing up as a kid in my birth town of Zorzor, Lofa County. It was forbidden by then to play any sports based on my parent's bizarre predisposition that athletes or players always end up becoming criminals or street children, even though they never convinced me by any argument. For them, playing any type of sports was not for successful people in life. So, for us (their children), the question of sports was completely ruled out.

Coping with such authoritarian measures as a kid with great soccer talent was an uphill battle. I attempted some days by conniving with my brothers or sisters to cover my tracks so that I could go and play just a little bit—say, for forty-five minutes—but the cost was always astronomically high. So, I respectfully disengaged, and eventually my parents won. My dream of becoming a football star or icon was shattered.

The field of sports has experienced a modern transformation. It has become an alluring focus fantastically attracting many young people. Athletes or players are among the highest paid celebs or stars in the world. Several of them receive mouthwatering and matchless salaries and allowances that continue to attract millions of kids and grown-ups to the field. The expansion and improvement of technology, various games themselves, and facilities have added great value to the field. Academies and specialized athletic institutions of learning with diverse specialties are being established globally to progressively develop the talent and potential of young people with the aim of transforming them into great assets for their personal development and the good of society in general. The development of sports is a revolution that has created a huge opportunity for young people who initially seemed to be a lost generation.

The world of sports in its many aspects is now home to hundreds of millions of brilliant and gifted young men and women. They have a wide range of options from which they can make great careers in soccer, basketball, volleyball, racing, track and field, swimming, wrestling, boxing, etc.

Their lives have tremendously changed, thus becoming models for their peers and generations to come.

All-time basketball legend Michael Jordan of the Chicago Bulls as of 2018 is worth $1.7 billion. Steph Curry of the Golden State Warriors has a net worth as of 2018 around $200 million and LeBron James, a star in Cleveland, Miami, and now Los Angeles, as of 2018 has a net worth of $400 million. Not only in the United States but across the world, countless young people in high schools, universities and colleges as well as professional organizations aspiring to be to be like these legends whom they see as their role models.

In soccer land, the all-time legend, King Pelé of Brazil, in 2018 has a net worth of $100 million. Juventus's Cristiano Ronaldo's net worth as of 2018 is $400 million. Neymar Junior of Brazil is worth $99.8 million, and Lionel Messi of Argentina has a net worth in 2018 of $80million.

Amazingly in Africa, the game of soccer has become a beacon of hope capturing the heart and soul of many talented young people. The love of the game and growing determination of the youth, mostly the less fortunate, into great football stars has attracted millions. A significant number of the world's wealthiest soccer legends are also from Africa, further indicating the public interest, growth, and development of the game. Indisputably, there are football icons on the continent whose achievements are worth emulating by this generation and others to come.

Cameroon's Samuel Eto'o Fils is currently the richest African soccer star. He is a legend whose worth was put at $202 million as of 2012. The former Cameroonian international has a delicate history that recounts outstanding football accomplishments in England, Spain, Russia, Italy, and Turkey. Like Nwankwo Kanu of Nigeria and Didier Drogba of Côte d'Ivoire, who have made astounding investments in their respective countries, Eto'o constructed and turned over to the government of Cameroon a modern health center, Laquinitie Hospital in the Duala region. The hospital is worth millions of dollars. Today, the hospital is a major referral health center in the Douala region of Cameroon.

Certainly, there are other legendary African soccer players on the continent whose fame and contributions remain conspicuously notable. From Côte d'Ivoire alone, you have great stars like Yaya Touré (in 2015 worth $170 million) and Didier Drogba ($155 million). Similarly, Nigeria boasts stars such as Jay-Jay Okocha ($150 million) and Nwankwo Kanu ($100 million). The former Nigerian internationals are greatly remembered for their leadership roles as captains in giving their country great successes in soccer history. Like Eto'o of Cameroon, the two Nigerian internationals are role models for their generation as well as those emerging.

Similarly, outstanding movie and theatrical performers have socially and culturally transformed society by effectively communicating thought-provoking and motivating messages through their spectacular dramatizations. Many of their performances are characteristic of exceptional cultural and traditional norms reflecting a diversified society. Of course, in their breathtaking and life-changing performances, they demonstrate passion and humanity.

It is clear that the cinema and theatrical arenas have facilitated a great paradigm shift that has stimulated cultural diversification. In the United States, for example, Tyler Perry's movies and television series have become a source of therapy and the promotion of a happy family life. Tyler is one of the ten richest movie actors in the world, with a 2018 net worth of $600 million.

Also in the United States, one of the world's best-known entertainers, Bill Cosby, has impacted the world greatly with his many years of hilarious but educative television series. Like Perry, Cosby is one of the ten richest movie actors in the world, as of 2018 worth $400 million. Perry and Cosby are just two of the hundreds of thousands of actors and performers who are living exemplary lives worth emulating.

It is worth noting that in spite of the Cosby's imprint of society, he was accused of sexual assault by Andrea Constand. This label has considerably affected high standing in society. On June 17, 2017, the judge in Cosby's case declared mistrial due to the failure of the jury to reach a unanimous verdict. This is just a tip of the iceberg of what celebs go through despite their apparent glamorous world.

Only during the 1990s did the movie industry in Africa begin to undergo a transition to modernity. The technology advanced, modern equipment was introduced, and the quality of casts improved significantly. By the 2000s, there was an extraordinary expansion and modernization of the industry attracting many young people and earning them prominence and a meaningful life. Rising from a poor and wretched life to stardom is an incredible opportunity that contributes to ending social burdens and human suffering.

Although there's still much to do to bring the African industry up to speed with the West; but throughout the continent, the cinema and the theater have become strategic gateways to success. Polished performances and the resulting fame are earning riches for those in the industries and raising their character and reputation as aspirational goals for millions. For example, Charlize Theron, a South African fashion model, actor, and producer, is the richest celebrity in that nation, with an estimated net worth of $110 million and ranked as South Africa's richest celebrity in 2018.

Similarly, in Nigeria, the number of rich celebs in the industry has sharply increased over the years. For example, Richard Mofe Damijo, a leading actor, is worth $15 million as of 2018. Desmond Elliot, another popular and passionate Nigerian movie star, has a net worth of $10 million since 2018. His kinsman and one of Africa's leading entertainers, John Okafor, affectionately known as Mr. Ibu, is worth $4.2 million as of 2018.

The number of celebs in Ghana is also rapidly increasing. Among the many Ghanaian stars notably becoming richer by the day are the actors Majid Michel ($1.6 million), Chris Attoh ($1.2 million), Yvonne Nels ($900,000), and Jackie Apiah ($800,000).

Absolutely, we can go on naming celebs and highlighting their wealth and fame for a long time. Every time a celeb comes to prominence, another is just starting to rise— meaning that in every sphere of life there are celebs.

Imagine talking about the lifelong achievements of a legend like the late Michael Jackson, who thrilled the world and remarkably swayed a whole generation to his unique culture. His striking lifestyle made every child want to become MJ, as he was globally known. The paradox is that even in non–English-speaking countries, the young and old craved the voice of MJ. His innovation and creativity deceived several emerging young convicts to believe that he was supernatural. For them, Michael was an immortal being who could simply disappear and reappear and thus could never die.

I was also drawn in by this myth that MJ was a spiritual being absolutely different from us. In fact, watching his irresistible video *Thriller* used to be a hilarious scene where I would distance myself from the movie screen, my slippers in my hands, ready to run. The scene at the cemetery, with veiled and well-masked figures rising from the graves and dancing, was for me the best moment, but the horror dimension always kept me running away. Dressed like Michael and learning to break-dance and moonwalk had no special designation and time. On the football pitch or running errands, whether in the backyard, in our rooms, or in school, we never stopped break-dancing or moonwalking.

Today, although MJ is dead, his lyrics live on. Before his death in 2009, he was said to have a net worth of $434 million. For Michael, it wasn't about how much money he earned but rather his worth was measured by his name which moved the entire world. Like Tupac Shakur whose legacy strongly lives in the hearts of young people, many still mythically doubt the death of Michael.

And then comes the name Whitney Houston. She rocked the world with her stunning and irresistible voice. She was a natural—an icon in her own class without a single reference to downcast moments. She represented glamour, elegance, uniqueness, and radiance. Whitney's musical wisdom astonished the world. She was deservedly named by Guinness World Records as the most awarded all-time female artist. She received hundreds of outstanding awards and sold more than 200 hundred million albums worldwide. Although her net worth before her death was put at $20 million, Whitney earned for herself a distinguished reputation that greatly impacted the world.

One voice that distinguished itself in the celebrity world and remains exceptional is that of the legendary American songwriter, singer, and pianist, Aretha Louis Franklin. Born to the civil rights activist Clarence L. Franklin in the United States in 1942, Aretha rose to fame as an outstanding character in US history. Clarence Franklin is remembered for organizing the historic 1963 Detroit Walk to Freedom ahead of his good friend Martin Luther King Jr.'s march on Washington. Aretha did not just become a music legend, but like her father, she raised her voice so firmly that it had great impact on the civil rights movement in the United States. In 1967, she released her famous song "Respect," which became an anthem for the racial and gender political movements of the time. Franklin is widely remembered for these few lines in her memoir, *Aretha: From These Roots*: "It reflected the need of a nation, the need of an average man and woman in the street, the businessman, the mother, the fireman, the teacher—everyone wanted respect," Franklin wrote. The song became one of the battle cries of the civil rights movement as it inspired, motivated and gave hope. She was a courageous freedom fighter; a mighty warrior who never wavered in the pursuit of social justice.

Aretha was a phenomenal woman with impressive accomplishments. In the musical world, she was known as the Queen of Soul; she lived in her own class. Her mix of soul-pop, R&B, and gospel was brilliant. Aretha won eighteen Grammy Awards and also became the first woman to be inducted into the Rock and Roll Hall of Fame. Aretha commanded great recognition and respect from American society, going beyond political and racial lines. Her advocacy and music brought Americans together irrespective of race and status. She was adored by everyone.

As ordinary as the circumstances of her birth, young Aretha rose with her natural charm and acumen to inspire a whole generation. Her exemplary life is a legacy of hope that unites in diversity. On August 16, 2018, the news of Aretha's death saddened the entire world, but her unfading memory lives on. In the immediate aftermath of her death, the Obamas tweeted, "She helped define the American experience. In her voice, we could feel our history, all of it and every shade – our light, our quest for redemption and our hard won respect. May the Queen of Souls rest in eternal peace."; John Legend, "Greatest vocalist I've ever known"; Elton John, "I adore her and worship her talent"; and Hillary Clinton, "You open our eyes, ears and hearts."

In spite of the peculiarities of the celebrity world, times have changed dramatically. From the 1970s to the 1990s, there were pouches of news about the few celebrities who ventured into the political waters of the United States. Some contested congressional, senatorial, mayoral, and council seats.

Most notable was the rise of the first celebrity to the presidency of the United States in 1981, Hollywood actor Ronald Reagan. President Reagan was elected to two terms as governor of California, beginning in 1967, and then elected president in 1981. He was one of Hollywood's outstanding actors from 1937 to 1964, with more than 50 movies to his credit. He co-starred in films with Humphrey Bogart, Bette Davis, and Errol Flynn. It is important to note however that Reagan was not just a regular celeb but a great statesman. He was a WWII veteran and famous conservative remembered for his economic theory known as "Reaganomics."

President Reagan is credited with helping to further redefine the purpose of government and pressuring the then Soviet Union to end the Cold War. In particular, Republicans remember President Reagan for solidifying the conservative agenda for decades after his presidency. His success as president was largely due to his diverse background, especially his deep conservative beliefs, valuable leadership characteristics, and experience cultivated during a lifetime.

In fact, ascending to the presidency and scoring milestones without such diversification would not have been possible for an ordinary Hollywood actor. Notwithstanding, he also represents a success story of the celebrity world. President Reagan's presidency in the United States, the mother of democracy, actually ended celebrity statesmanship in 1989 until the 2000s.

Indeed, the 2000s represent the epoch that ushered in the spontaneous rise of celebrities to political leadership. Interestingly, politics was rarely associated with celebrities' line of business. This dramatic shift is a crucial groundbreaking moment that has implications for the future of democracy. Across Africa, Europe, Asia and the United States a steady wave of celebrities are competing to become heads of state as well as in congressional (or parliamentary or legislative) elections.

This dramatic change has been widely viewed by pundits as a grave menace that could undermine the advancement of democracy, given the gap between stardom and political leadership or governance. Politics or political leadership has always been a field for men and women well prepared, with the requisite knowledge and experience in corporate or political governance. This relation cannot be accidental, and we propose to unravel the possible implications for democratic governance of the present upsurge in celebrity aspirants.

In 2003, the legendary movie star, Arnold Schwarzenegger, was elected governor of California. Schwarzenegger was a renowned action movie superstar and body builder, world-famous for his role in the movie, *The Terminator*. The former California governor once asserted, "I would run for president if my foreign birth requirement didn't prevent me from doing so."

The bizarre reality of this ambitious intent to run for president is highlighted by the findings of the watchdog group Citizens for Responsibility and Ethics in Washington (CREW), which named Schwarzenegger as one of the worst governors in US history. CREW clearly addresses the former governor's limited understanding of political governance despite his successful celebrity career. One can vividly see that his limited or nonexistent experience in corporate or political leadership caused the reported failure in his governorship.

In the Philippines, you have one man, Manny Pacquiao, who is a boxer, actor, and musician turned politician. Pacquiao has a peculiar profile. He is considered as one of the greatest and most influential personalities in the Philippines and the world. In May 2010, Pacquiao was elected to the House of Representatives in the Fifteenth Congress of the Philippines. It took him two tries to be elected. He was beaten by Darlene Antonio-Custodio in his first attempt in 2007 before his second attempt could see him through to the position.

In 2016, Pacquiao was again elected Senator. It is however important to note that whether or not the Filipino citizens wanted to see him in the ring more than in the court for which he was elected, they were convinced by his entertaining and kind nature that his recent election proves he can do both. Sure, that's who this celeb is; a kind entertainer—something that largely formed the basis for his election by the Filipinos.

Consistent with Pacquiao's ten remarkable accomplishments; boxing, music and acting account for nine while his political achievement only references his successive elections to the House of Representatives and Senate of the Philippines. His political achievement does not detail any specifics with regard to leadership dynamism and achievements, further suggesting that Pacquiao was basically elected on the basis of his fame.

This is how one pundit put it: "His ability to destroy opponents with a single punch in contrast to his easy-going personality is that of a true champion who loves to give the fans what they want while being successful in every meaning of the word." So Pacquiao basically sustained his support base by his performance in the ring, the cinema, or the stage.

Also caught up by the political-celebrity wind, the Haitian American hip-hop superstar, Wyclef Jean, took advantage of his popularity to give the 2010 presidential election in his country a shot. Wyclef was optimistic that his popularity would land him the country's highest seat. To his deep surprise, he was disqualified for not meeting the residency requirements immediately following his completion of the registration process. Who knows? Probably, Wyclef would have won that election based on his popularity, had he qualified to run.

In Africa, Senegalese Grammy-winning singer, percussionist, and composer Youssou N'dour added his name to the list of celebs seeking political power. Youssou sought to unseat eighty-year-old Abdoulaye Wade. He lost that election in the first round, however, and supported the presidential bid of Macky Sall, who defeated Wade to win the election. In what appears to be a payback for his support, Youssou was appointed by President Sall as minister of culture and tourism.

The musical star is also a successful businessman and owns a newspaper as well as a radio and television station in Senegal. Youssou has taken Senegal's popular *mbalax* music to a worldwide audience. This portfolio, especially his influence, gives cause for politicians to be mindful that in spite of his loss in the 2012 election, he firmly has his eyes on the Dakar mayoral position and the presidency.

Then came also one of the biggest surprises ever in the history of political leadership. In the United States, the election of the reality television star and real estate mogul Donald Trump to the presidency of the free world in 2016 was greeted with mixed reactions. Many people expressed utter shock that a candidate whose entire campaign was plagued by the worst controversies ever in US electoral history could be voted to the Oval Office.

Furthermore, the defeat of his opponent, Mrs. Hillary Clinton, who was deemed the most qualified of all the candidates who participated in that election, based on her wide experience and impeccable credentials, left pundits with the conclusion that Trump's victory was a mystery. There was no doubt that Mrs. Clinton's huge approval ratings over Trump at home and abroad, as revealed by credible pollsters on the margins of the election, convinced many people that she was the favorite candidate to win the election.

Mr. Trump is on record for stooping lower than any American presidential candidate by reason of his immoral statements, mockery, and bullying tactics. The *Independent News* and the *New York Times* were able to compile ten of his despicable actions. Candidate Trump mocked a *New York Times* disabled reporter, Serge Kavaski, when he attempted answering a question at a campaign rally. The scene was horrible.

Disgustingly, Trump was caught on camera bragging about sexual assaults on women. This is exactly what he had to say: "You know I'm automatically attracted to beautiful—I just start kissing them. It's like a magnet. Just kiss. I don't even wait. And when you're a star, they let you do it, you can do anything. Grab them by the p***y, you can do anything."

One of his campaign messages that was believed to have resonated very well with his Republican base was the awful characterization of Mexicans: "They're bringing drugs, they're bringing crime, they're rapists …."

In response to CNN's news anchor Don Lemon on the question of the 2014 *Fusion* article which averred that 80 percent of Central American migrant women passing through Mexico are raped, Trump argued by inference that once the rape occurred in Mexico, then Mexicans coming to the United States are automatically rapists. Don Lemon's efforts to convince candidate Trump that the rape report story by *Fusion* cannot be used to justify his claims of rape, drug trafficking, and crime attributable to Mexicans proved unsuccessful.

Donald Trump incited physical violence at his campaign rallies. It was unimaginable for well-meaning Americans and others around the world that a presidential candidate of the Free World would provoke violence of any sort and measure. Trump to his supporters: "If you see somebody getting ready to throw a tomato, knock the crap out of 'em, would you? Seriously. Okay? Just knock the hell—I promise you, I will pay for the legal fees. I promise. I promise."

It became evident during the campaign that candidate Trump's intolerance to Muslims is unprecedentedly high. Even now, as president of the United States, he demonstrates that intolerance with pride. During the election, Khizr and Ghazala Khan were invited to the 2016 Democratic National Convention, and Khizr gave an impassioned speech about his son, Humayun S. M. Khan, who died in combat when deployed to Iraq in 2004. The speech greatly criticized Trump's intolerance to Muslims. Trump replied by implying that Ghazala hadn't been permitted to talk, and this is exactly what he had to say: "His wife, if you look at his wife, she was standing there. She had nothing to say. She probably ... maybe she wasn't allowed to have anything to say. You tell me, but plenty of people are saying that. She was extremely quiet. And it looked like she had nothing to say." Trump's disdainful description of Mrs. Khan's silence was inconceivable, especially one by an American presidential candidate to a Gold Star Mother.

Candidate Trump persistently called for a ban on Muslims entering the country, which many pundits believed resonated with his Republican base. President Trump succeeded in banning refugees and citizens of seven Muslim countries from coming to the United States, despite stiff opposition from the American public. The countries are Iran, Libya, Somalia, Syria, Yemen, North Korea, and Venezuelan officials (in the version upheld by the Supreme Court in June 2018). This decision remains very unpopular especially among Democrats and moderate conservatives who seriously criticized the president's decision as un-American. They claim the decision is divisive and undemocratic. Thus, it does not represent the values of the United States.

Megyn Kelly, an American journalist of NBC and formerly of Fox News from 2004 to 2017, moderated one of the Republican primary candidates' debates in which Trump participated. Kelly posed a tough question to him regarding his attitude about women, and he later claimed that she gave him a grilling because she was on her period: "There was … blood coming out of her wherever." It was a sickening scene. The irony was that the more Trump hammered those abhorrent comments, the more his support soared and the more he spewed despicable comments.

Trump's insatiable sexual appetite was also unraveled during the 2016 election campaign season. He has been persistently accused of sexual harassment, assault, and misconduct. It was conspicuously and convincingly demonstrated on countless occasions during the elections. In addition to multiple sexual assault accusations and lawsuits filed against Trump, two notable instances caught the attention of the world. This obsession led him to seek assurances frequently from strangers that he had beautiful women in his life.

Candidate Trump made downright creepy sexual statements about his own daughter Ivanka. During the 1997 Miss Teen USA pageant, he sat in the audience as Ivanka, herself still a teenager, helped host the event from onstage. He turned to Brook Antoinette Mahealani Lee, Miss Universe at the time, and asked for her opinion of his daughter's body. Trump to Lee: "Don't you think my daughter's hot? She's hot, right?"

Ms. Lee recalled her reaction: "I was like, 'Really?' That's just weird. She was sixteen. That's creepy." Certainly, it all adds up to a scene of insanity. One's imagination would simply be a theatrical reality where a sexually woozy beast without heart seeks to devour its own flesh.

In similar scenario, Candidate Trump made eerie comments about Paris Hilton. "Now, somebody who a lot of people don't give credit to but in actuality is really beautiful is Paris Hilton. I've known Paris Hilton from the time she's twelve. Her parents are friends of mine, and the first time I saw her she walked into a room and I said, 'Who the hell is that? I would date her after ten years.'" Such sexually haunted comments about a teenage girl are both outrageous and intolerable. But again, if the crocodile can imagine eating its own flesh, then what about eating the flesh of a frog?

It is absurd that even in the face of being confronted by more sexual assault accusations and lawsuits than any candidate or president of the United States, Trump is still president. Interestingly, many others with far fewer such accusations did face harsh consequences.

This is the thing. Trump rose to power as a popular celebrity, deemed to be a billionaire, and understandably embroiled with many perhaps shady financial deals. The latest Forbes list of the world's billionaires puts Trump's worth at $3.1 billion in 2018. Trump's connections with Russian President Vladimir Putin and his failure to disclose his tax returns during the campaign go far to justify some of the suspicions about his dealings. The president of the United States is being investigated on allegations of collusion with Russia to win the 2016 presidential election, leaving many with the impression that he did not fairly win the election that took him to the most powerful office in the world.

Another dimension of the controversial United States president is that his display of bullying, bigotry, and arrogance, along with his misrepresentations and inconsistencies, is unprecedented in American political history. This trend has persisted from Trump's campaign. It is not just bizarre but also worrisome that the most powerful person in the world virtually symbolizes division. President Trump's attacks know no bounds. Nearly anyone—children, the disabled, women, celebrities, professionals in various spheres, politicians, and poverty-stricken migrants—can be the targets of his mockery, bullying, and outright lies.

One notable name that may never disappear from Trump's vocabulary is Obama. He knows the name and the man himself very well, but ironically, Trump prefers to choose the path of hatred for Obama. This hatred is demonstrated by all manner of attacks on the former president. He points to Obama for almost everything that is negative and has sought to undo major decisions or deals instituted by the Obama administration. Trump pulled the United States out of the Trans-Pacific Partnership (TPP) and the historic Iranian deals consummated by President Obama's administration. These unpopular actions of the president put the United States at a disadvantage, giving China a leadership role in the TPP and setting back efforts to get Iran to abandon its nuclear quest. President Trump's persistent attacks on US alliances, notably the G7, NATO, and the EU, are incomprehensible. In particular, he does it and then makes common cause with the worst adversaries of his own nation, North Korea and Russia.

Despite repeated failures, President Trump's biggest dream is to repeal Obamacare, but sadly he has no credible replacement. For him, it's about eroding Obama's legacy and not guaranteeing healthcare for more than twenty million Americans. Erratically, he accused Obama of being the architect of ISIS; being weak on borders thus creating a floodgate for illegal immigrants to come to America; acting with weakness and indecision in handling the Syria war; and leaving the economy in a bad state. Fact-checking these claims makes Trump more of a comedian than president. It is really disheartening when the one who is supposed to be the most powerful leader in the world is the best liar.

The president's unprecedented policy shifts toward US allies have caused serious apprehensions among Americans. Many have disparaging concerns about how President Trump is playing to the gallery of the Russian president. Pundits have opined that the president's actions have implications for the security of the United States.

Trump's government has recorded the highest turnover compared to any of his predecessors. In eighteen months of his administration, more than a dozen senior officials of his government have resigned, signifying his inability to provide decent and productive leadership. His government lacks basic organization and is embroiled with lies, inconsistencies, and harsh policies.

The *Washington Post* Fact Checker newsletter examined the president's statements and reported on NBC News that in 558 days of his presidency, Trump had made 4,229 misleading claims. The Fact Checker also reported that

President Trump makes an average of 7.6 lies every day. On another note, President Trump is faced with a criminal investigation on alleged collusion with Russia during the 2016 campaign as well as multiple sexual assault and misconduct cases. For a sitting president of the United States to be embroiled with so many criminal and civil investigations and such a web of controversies is completely demeaning. Serious doubts have arisen as to the integrity and credibility of Trump himself as well as the presidency of the United States.

President Trump's questionable leadership style is not a surprise because he rose to the office as an outsider to the political basics of Washington. Even though he ran on the Republican Party's ticket, it is clear that the president's erratic leadership style does not square with conservative principles. Still, Republicans are compelled to stick with him, no matter the harshness or unpopularity of his policies, because of the support he enjoys from his base. It seems that opposing Trump puts an elected Republican official at risk with supporters, except for those who would stand their ground and don't care about Trump's retaliation. Members of the president's cabinet and Republicans in Congress are very mindful of how they approach or react to his policies. The risk of staying silent about the continuous chaos created by Trump in the Oval Office is that many Republicans will go down with the president if his party's alleged collusion with Russia turns out to be true and punishable by law.

Eventually, their failure to stand up to Trump in the face of his erratic leadership style, especially the radical change he's effecting in the Republican Party, has implications for their credibility, which could result in many of them losing their seats in Congress for the November 2018 midterm elections.

Pundits have strongly warned that the president's arbitrary leadership style and web of controversies are eroding America's age-old legacy of being the mother of democracy.

President Trump's real nature, it seems, is his inner "strongman," an apparently intrinsic characteristic that explains his admiration for dictators like Kim Jong-un of North Korea, Vladimir Putin of Russia, Rodrigo Duterte of the Philippines, and Recep Tayyip Erdogan of Turkey. He has his own dictatorial tendencies. He believes in making unilateral decisions, taking credit for every good thing that happens, and disowning negative developments, like any other strongman-style leader. He hates critical or opposing views about his questionable actions. Obviously, these are features of a tyrant, and it is truly incomprehensible that the president of the free world freely displays such characteristics. It should not surprise anyone that President

Trump feels comfortable in chaos, as evidenced by the current chaotic nature of his leadership.

As of now, the president's former campaign chairman, Paul Manafort, has been found guilty of eight counts of tax and bank fraud, which will likely result in years of prison time. Trump's personal lawyer and fixer, Michael Cohen, has also pleaded guilty to crimes of breaking tax, bank fraud, and campaign finance laws. Cohen's plea also implicated Trump in federal campaign finance violations.

Prior to the Manafort and Cohen legal debacles, three of the president's men also pleaded guilty for their involvement with Russia during the 2016 elections. Special Counsel Robert Mueller's inquiry into alleged Russia interference in the 2016 election charged Michael Flynn, George Papadopoulos, and Rick Gates. Flynn, Trump's national security adviser, pleaded guilty on one count of lying to the FBI. George Papadopoulos, Trump's foreign policy adviser, pleaded guilty of lying to the FBI about his contacts with Russia. And Richard Gates, Trump's former deputy campaign manager, also pleaded guilty of lying to FBI about his contacts with Russia during the 2016 campaign. In essence, President Trump is surrounded by criminals.

With a criminal investigation of this magnitude involving the president himself, the future of his presidency is at risk. Although his actions continue to embolden his base, they cannot continue unabated because they contravene the ideals of the great United States. Sadly, America's hard-earned pride as the land of possibilities and the beacon of hope is unjustly paying for Trump's erratic governance model.

Notwithstanding that celebrities do have positive life-changing impact on society, it is worth noting that their peculiar lifestyles are completely unrelated to political governance. Of course, stardom and politics are two old but distinct traditions. In particular, it has become increasingly clear that celebrities who have no credible corporate or political leadership experience when given political power are likely to underperform or create setbacks in their leadership. President Donald Trump of the United States and President George Oppong Manneh Weah of Liberia are very good examples.

In less than twenty-four months of their respective leadership, democracy has come under serious assault by reason of their erratic and tyrannical approach to governance. In Trump's America and Weah's Liberia, hate, acrimony, and division are quickly taking root as never before. The future of democracy in the two countries is uncertain as free speech, human rights, freedom of the press, and the rule of law are being seriously undermined and eventually endangered.

On the other hand, celebrities with leadership experience in either the corporate or the political sphere are likely to perform well. This scenario may seem infrequent, but former President Ronald Reagan of the United States is a classic example. He rose from being an outstanding Hollywood actor to the American presidency and is remembered as one of America's best presidents. In essence, the leadership of President Trump of the United States in the Western world and that of President Weah of Liberia in Africa are excellent demonstrations that celebrity leadership is more likely to pose a threat to democratic governance.

However, the two scenarios are very dissimilar. The United States has credible democratic institutions and systems capable of exposing and rejecting any forms of antidemocratic practice. So, despite the current uncertainties in the United States about the future of their democracy created by Trump's government, Americans are still hopeful of dealing with the situation and returning to the path of democratic governance. Unlike the United States, Liberia is a poor and war-ravaged nation still struggling to deal with the scars of the war. The country has weak democratic institutions. Justice is still in short supply, corruption is pervasive, and impunity remains entrenched. With the current threat the country faces in terms of the assault on its emerging democracy and the lack of will demonstrated so far by the Weah government to act appropriately, Liberians are apprehensive about the peace and stability of their country.

Chapter 3

The Journey to Stardom

Parallel with the United States' experience with the election of a reality TV star, President Donald J. Trump Sr., Liberia experienced a rude awakening on December 26, 2017, with the election of a soccer star, George Oppong Manneh Weah, as president.

The election of these two celebrities may be the two biggest political shocks so far in democratic history. President Weah's unbelievable journey—from the slums of Monrovia to become one of the world's best soccer stars and then president of Liberia—requires close attention. Every effort has to be made in unraveling the implications of this strange political phenomenon for Liberia's fragile democracy.

In the small West African nation of Liberia, George Oppong Manneh Weah was born in the Clara Town community on October 1, 1966. Clara Town is a slum community of Bushrod Island, a major suburb of Monrovia,

Liberia's capital. Weah's father, William T. Weah Sr., was a carpenter, and his mother, Anna Quaye Weah, was a market woman.

George Weah was raised by his paternal grandmother, Emma Klonjlaleh Brown, when his mother and father separated. He attended middle school at the Muslim Congress High School and then matriculated to the Wells Hairston High School in Monrovia but dropped out in the final year of his studies with a focus on playing football.

Weah was a talented youngster with a special discernment in soccer that made his performance extraordinary. Although he came from an extremely poor family, he was naturally loved by communities in which he played. At age fifteen, young Weah was already a figure of attraction. He played for the Survivor Youth Football Club in Montserrado from 1981 to 1984.

Weah's fantastic display at Young Survivor landed him in central Liberia, Bong County, where he played for one of the leading soccer clubs in the region, the Bong Range Football Club. Bong Range was based in the rich mining area of Bong Mines, and as expected, Weah did not disappoint, offering his very best. Like Young Survivor, he spent a year at Bong Range, from 1984 to 1985. The rapid exposure of the skillful young man put him in the spotlight, and eventually he was an attractive potential player for the leading soccer clubs in the national soccer league.

With Weah's strong determination to play soccer at a professional level, he did not return to school following the end of his youth career at the Young Survivor and Bong Range football clubs. As a young man without guidance in his fast-developing career, he also got distracted by a temporary job at the Liberia Telecommunication Corporation (LTC), where he served as switchboard technician. Weah's service at the LTC was brief as the pressure on him intensified to join one of the leading clubs in the country, Mighty Barrolle Football Club.

Mighty Barrolle and Invincible Eleven Majesty soccer clubs were the two football giants in the Liberian domestic league. Young Weah's introduction on the national scene set the stage for his journey to stardom. He only spent a year at Mighty Barrolle and left in 1986 to join the Invincible Eleven Majesty club; he left there in 1987. Weah's unmatched performance in the domestic league, for the two leading clubs in the country, showed that his speed, accuracy, and skills were ready for an international career. Before long, he would be a dominant player on the world stage. He would bring out the act of "Weahism," satiate the quest of an entire generation, and make football more lovable than ever before.

From Invincible Eleven in Liberia, Weah found himself in Côte d'Ivoire, where he played briefly for Africa Sports of Abidjan before joining Tonnerre football club in Yaoundé,

Cameroon, in 1987. He had successful times in Abidjan and Yaoundé. In particular, Yaoundé is seen as the springboard that landed him Europe.

Excelling in soccer was no longer a question for Weah. During the short time he spent in Cameroon, he performed beyond expectation and earned his first European contract with A. S. Monaco of France. Certainly, it was Arsene Wenger, then coach of A. S. Monaco who facilitated Weah's entry into the international soccer arena.

Certainly, Weah has honored and recognized Mr. Wenger in various respects. His deep appreciation for the astute soccer manager proves worthy of the role Wenger played in his life. The pep talks, advice, and trusted guidance transcended the role of an ordinary coach. Thus, Weah has long averred that he considers Wenger to be a mentor.

Weah was inspired and prepared to give France and the world a spectacle of wonders. He played for Monaco from 1988 to 1992. Those years were characterized by great successes. While in France, Weah also played for Paris Saint-Germain for three years and was no less spectacular.

Still in Europe, he moved to Italy, where he also had a great time of his career. Weah played for A C Milan for five years from 1995 to 2000. As in France, Weah's record was incomparable. Just within one year in 2000, he played for Chelsea and Manchester City.

Toward the end of 2000, Weah moved back to France, where he played for Marseille up to 2001. Then, between 2000 and 2003, he played for Al Jazira in the United Arab Emirates (UAE). Weah's outstanding accomplishments stunned the world, and he has gone down in soccer history as an indisputable legend.

Judging by the measure of FIFA's characterization, Weah deserves all of the accolades for an icon of his statue. That is why it is no surprise or mistake that he has rightfully received his flowers while still alive. He was recognized across the world in every way. He received titles like humanitarian, ambassador, and best footballer, among many others, based on his soccer accomplishments.

Twice, in 1989 and 1994, Weah received the African Footballer of the Year Award. In 1995, he received FIFA's Ballon d'Or and FIFA World Player of the Year Award, even though he had no record of playing in the World Cup. Weah also received the European Footballer of the Year Award in 1996. Although he merited this award, winning it as the first and only non-European so far remains a subject of concern for many pundits and enthusiasts. That was extraordinary, and the accomplishment put him in a special category of soccer history.

The football legend also received other awards, including the Arthur Ashe Courage Award in 2004 and the Confederation of African Football (CAF) Legend Award in 2005. He also received the CAF 2018 Platinum Award following his election as president of Liberia. His wife, Mrs. Clar Weah, accepted the award in Marrakesh, Morocco, on his behalf. It is also notable that in 1997, UNICEF named Weah as its goodwill ambassador.

In spite of these great achievements, the journey wasn't all rosy. Weah also had his ups and downs. One such bad moment came when he was banned from six European matches for breaking the nose of Portuguese defender Jorge Costa on October 20, 1996. Weah said he couldn't stand the racist taunting from Costa during his team's two Champion League matches against FC Porto. The ban was the severest punishment Weah ever received during his entire international career. Thus, it was a moment of serious reflection for him as he continued to aspire to greatness in his God-given field.

A crucial dimension of Weah's career was his role in projecting his country's national team, the Lone Star. It is worth mentioning that the Liberian international soccer star played for his country's national team for twenty years from 1987 to 2007. Weah was an inspiration to the national team. His presence on the team encouraged his teammates to give their best.

Weah's colleagues on the team eagerly looked to him for leadership and to create a pathway to advance their careers just as he had. Their expectations were very high, but the reality was that they had to convincingly perform to meet the standards of overseas clubs, especially those in Europe. The simple fact was that whether or not Weah personally made connections for them, his display of professionalism and good character smoothed the way for Liberian players with similar qualities.

Few of Weah's colleagues made it to the international scene on their own merits, even though Weah's credentials served as a general recommendation for them to some extent. The likes of James "Salinsa" Debah made his way to Paris Saint-Germain in France and later to Panathinaikos in Greece. Prince Daye secured a great contract with Bastia in France. Christopher Wleh earned a contract with Arsenal in England. He was part of the Arsenal team that won the Premier League title in 1997 and again in 1998.

Similarly, Oliver Makor made it to Greece, where he played for Olimpiacos. One of the nation's best goalkeepers, Lewis Crayton played his professional soccer in the Netherlands for Grasshopper soccer club. One of the team's leading strikers, Frank "Jean" Seator, also played for Esperance in Tunisia before heading to Malaysia, where he played for Perak FC for the greater part of his career.

The international exposure of these players earned for them great careers and also promoted the reputation of the national team. Their exposure and professionalism, along with the presence of Weah, account for the successes of the national team by then. They are all credited for the pride they brought to the nation.

The days of Weah and teammates are considered the heyday of Liberian soccer history. They qualified for and participated in the 2003 Africa Nations Cup in Mali. It was a historic moment because it was the country's first qualification and participation in the continent's most prestigious soccer tourney.

During that same time, the national team of Liberia came close to qualifying for the 2002 FIFA World Cup. The national team simply needed a draw with a second-tier Ghanaian team, predominantly made up of local players, to make history by qualifying for the World Cup for the first time. Without doubt, Liberia would have pulled a great surprise at that World Cup with the caliber of players the country had, the coherence with which they played, and their determination to excel.

The stage was set, and the optimism both in Nigeria and the world at large, soared, as shown by the huge presence in the country of the international media and representatives of world and regional soccer bodies to witness that history-making event. In fact, the Ghanaians demonstrated their disregard for such a crucial match for Liberia by featuring an entirely second-tier Black Star team, making Liberia's qualification obvious.

To the dismay of an enthusiastic Liberian citizenry and the world, the Lone Star team headed by Weah, with its first choice of players who had defeated the first choice of Ghana Black Stars in Accra 3–1, lost to an underdog Ghanaian side 2–1. That match remains a mystery in Liberia's soccer history. George Weah's role as a coach and most senior player at the time remained questionable.

Weah deployed the faulty strategy of using one striker at the top and substituting for the only striker, the late Frank Seator, who made magical efforts. Weah himself on a number of occasions had one-on-one situations with an inexperienced Ghanaian goalkeeper but failed to score on any of those opportunities. Those actions of Mr. Weah on the football pitch were deplored by thousands of fans, who screamed for a change of strategy but to no avail.

The nation was disappointed in Weah and colleagues, for they had no justification for succumbing to that Ghanaian team, especially in such a crucial match. Even the Ghanaians seemed disappointed in Liberia for failing to qualify. The international media bliss and global attraction became meaningless. There was anger, frustration, and complete dissatisfaction throughout the nation. Weah became the subject of rage and was even accused of compromising the game and robbing Liberia of a golden chance. Whether or not the allegation against Weah was true, the fact was that a bleak future awaited his struggling colleagues in their pursuit of successful careers.

In fact, it was widely speculated that Weah was used by certain Western capitals to prevent the country from qualifying for the World Cup because, according to those speculations, doing so would increase the popularity of Mr. Charles Taylor, who was president at the time. According to the rumors, such an achievement would strengthen and improve Mr. Taylor's approval ratings domestically and project him as a productive leader, contrary to the perception of the West about his role in the civil war and his dictatorial tendencies. Weah faced a serious crisis of trust and confidence; his credibility eroded, and his face remained hidden.

Mr. Taylor too was hurt and angry, especially in the aftermath of all the investments his government had made to ensure that the team qualified. Mr. Taylor's government paid $5,000 to each foreign-based player for each qualifying match. His government also empowered the Liberia Football Association to ensure that plane tickets and hotel bills were always paid on time to ensure that professional players would arrive on time, both in Nigeria and abroad, to honor their matches. That was a great investment.

Mr. Taylor and his government did not take kindly to that loss. That was exactly when Mr. Taylor hinted that Weah wanted to be president of Liberia. Probably, from where he sat as president, he was well situated to have gotten the real story behind the Weah-Lone Star team's failure to qualify for the World Cup.

Interestingly, the firestorm turned to President Taylor vindicating Weah. The president's pronouncement that Weah was eyeing the presidency ironically rendered Weah blameless because many of the citizens inferred that Mr. Taylor had sinister motives. They claimed that the president was after Weah's life—a rumor that spread widely enough to erase the perceived betrayal by Weah and his colleagues and soothe the nation's pain.

Indeed, it was an interesting time. Whatever Weah did consciously, the loss did happen, and Liberia failed to qualify. It's a painful history that Liberians do not like to recount.

That failure had a serious psychological effect on the players to the extent that the team performed so badly at the African Nations Cup in Mali that as a direct consequence, the team failed to advance from the group stage to the round of sixteen. The early exit from the continent's prestigious tournament actually closed the chapter for that generation of players, except for Weah and a few of his colleagues who returned to Europe to resume their professional football career. The drama that ensued is that relations between Weah and many of his colleagues never rekindled so easily.

Sadly, many of the players were unable to keep their contracts. They had no options but to return home. They have all declined unbelievably. Notable among those professional players were James "Salinsa" Debah, Prince Daye, Oliver Makor, Christopher Wleh, Dionysius Segbwe, Jonathan "Boye Charles" Segbwe, Joe "Thunder" Nagbe, Zizi Roberts, and the goalkeeper Lewis Crayton.

A host of others played for clubs in Asia and the United Arab Emirates but couldn't keep their contracts either. They all had to return home. The Segbwe brothers— Dionysius, Jonathan, and Kelvin—have been serving government functions. Additionally, James Debah, who played professional football in France and Greece, had the opportunity of serving as head coach of the national team, the Lone Star. He was appointed by the president of the Liberia Football Association, Musa Bility, in November 2014, alongside former resourceful players including Midfield "Maestro" Kelvin Segbwe, Joe "Thunder" Nagbe, Thomas Kojo, and George Gebro. Debah and his technical team had the responsibility of building a new national team to properly replace the George Weah–led Lone Star team.

Unfortunately, Coach Debah and his technical crew failed to produce a befitting national team, for which they were charged. In fact, the team they managed failed to qualify for any tournament, including the World Cup and Africa Nations Cup. Today, George Weah and his generation of players are still haunted by the ghost of the historic Liberia versus Ghana 2002 World Cup qualifying match.

Like many men, George Weah has also experienced some challenges in his family life. He has been married for twenty years to Clar Weah, a Jamaican. They have three children; George Jr., Timothy, and Tita. Weah also has two other children outside of wedlock by two publicly known women, Meapeh Gono and MacDella Cooper.

In 2016, Weah was also the subject of a child abandonment case in the United States. The news about the soccer player fueled debates at major gatherings in Liberia as well as Liberian communities in the United States and elsewhere. Many of his fans argued that Weah's action was something that befalls any man. This defense did not seem solid enough to justify Weah's action. Many others viewed the action of a global soccer icon to abandon his own child as deliberate and irresponsible.

The debate automatically came to an end when Judge Eugene Bolton of the Newton County Civil Law Court in the State of Georgia ruled in the child abandonment case (File No. 2016CV239-1) that George Oppong Manneh Weah was the biological father of a ten-year-old child and instructed him to pay US$1,000 (one thousand United States dollars) per month pending further order.

Like his incredible rise to stardom, Weah's educational sojourn was unique. In preparation for his race to the

Liberian presidency, Weah was said to have bought a fake degree. But when it backfired and was posted on his very first campaign website, www.friendsofgeorgeweah.com, the story spread like wildfire and proved an embarrassment to Weah. Many national and international media institutions spread the story, to his detriment. Some indicated that Weah had committed a fraud and must therefore be prosecuted, while others suggested that he was a victim of a scam. The fact remains that purchasing an academic degree that you did not earn is criminal. One person who weighed in on the Weah diploma scandal was David Goldenberg, who wrote:

> "George Weah in Diploma-Mill Scandal
> For the African Footballer of the century, the Liberian Presidency is no longer a shot.
>
> Now that Weah has changed his mind and decided to enter the 22-man race for the presidency in October, 2005 that landslide no longer seems inevitable. If Weah is to win, he will have to overcome the scandal that is unfolding about his educational background—no small irony, considering how negligible the issue is compared to the deep woes enveloping Liberia as it emerges from 14 years of civil war. His campaign website   www.friendsofgeorgeweah.com

states that he received his bachelor's degree in Sports Management from Parkwood University in London. This is not a legitimate degree. Parkwood University was shut down by the Federal Trade Commission in 2003 because its owners, among other things, were marketing and selling "phony diplomas issued by fictitious universities via unsolicited commercial email and the Internet.

In other words, Weah's BA comes from a diploma mill that finds "students" with spam, sells them fake degrees, and has never had teachers, buildings, or classes, according to the FTC and published reports. Parkwood University was one of dozens of fake colleges and universities run by the University Degree Program, which at its peak was pulling in over $500,000 a month from degree seekers and may have cleared over $100 million.

George Gollin, a physics professor at the University of Illinois-Champaign, compiled a lengthy presentation on what he termed whack-a-gopher UDP university sites—sites that borrow wording liberally from one another and from real schools, so that when one fraud is uncovered, it can easily be replaced by another. The old Parkwood website is gone, but other UPD sites are still functional today."

Interestingly, on April 13, 2005, the *Liberian Observer* published the first article casting doubt on Weah's Parkwood degree. The newspaper investigated the university and discovered its failings.

Weah's press office claimed to have no idea how the degree appeared on the website, and the paper used the generous phrasing that Weah might have "fallen prey" to a bogus diploma scam, though it's hard to see how one could fall prey to any scheme that awarded a person a bachelor's degree for no work. It was also unclear when Weah first obtained the bachelor's degree or when it was first uploaded on his website. The first mention of it was made in November 2004, a year before the elections, ironically from a supporter extolling Weah's educational achievement.

Indeed, Weah bought the degree in the first place. After all, his lack of education was his biggest obstacle in ascending to the presidency. He became object of a typical bluster: How could anyone with such educational limitations decide on the best educational system for the people? How would he sell Liberia to the world when in fact he lacked the eloquence to be heard?

The then-chairman of Weah's party, Congress for Democratic Change, L. Orishall Gould, was interviewed. Displaying the common deception and hypocrisy of Liberian politics, Gould took a complicated line in the interview, defending Weah's degree while conceding that Parkwood might be suspect as an institution. He took the stance that the issue was unimportant and would not affect the election.

"He acquired a bachelor's in sports administration," Gould said. "It was a regular full-year program. It was very intensive. It was also accelerated, but included all the regular courses you would do to obtain a bachelor's." He also attempted to reframe Weah's critics as claiming that the subject of his degree was the issue rather than its source. "How can a geologist who studied rocks say he is more educated than [someone with a degree in] sports management?" Gould asked. "How can an accountant say he is more educated than a lawyer?"

This was just the tip of the iceberg, unveiling a fake political architecture that was constructed by Weah and his team of schemers to hijack political power to enrich themselves at the expense of an already poverty-ridden and war-wearied citizenry. Ironically, Chairman Gould became a victim of the cartel he contributed to nurturing. He was brutally kicked out of the CDC at one of its many orchestrated primaries and had to run for his life in Tubmanburg, Bomi County. Like Moses, he saw the promised land from a distance but did not enter it.

Understandably, Weah did not mention his fake degree story by any measure knowing it would have backfired when he participated in the 2005 elections. In any event, the major negative campaign against him from the opposition was that he lacked the proper education to lead the country.

By then, Weah did not have a high school certificate or diploma as required while seeking the highest office in the land. His confession on a local talk show on Radio Veritas instantly crushed the enthusiasm of many of his supporters and eventually weakened his entire campaign. Radio Veritas was one of the local radio stations widely listened to by then. It was an odd confession by Weah, and the criticism from his opponents seriously paralyzed his presidential bid. Consequently, he lost that election to Madam Ellen Johnson Sirleaf in a runoff election in November 2005.

Inconsistently, after Weah and his supporters had consistently maintained that education was not a necessary requirement for one seeking the presidency, this is what he had to say following his defeat in the 2005 election: "Education is a continual process. It's like a bicycle: if you don't pedal, you don't go forward."

Weah's reawakening following the 2005 shock unveiled a more determined candidate, readier to pursue education, which he had rejected as the ultimate essential element for success. Word was that Weah returned to high school and obtained a diploma at age forty and went on to DeVry University in Florida, where he obtained a bachelor's degree in business management.

Similarly, in 2011, Weah was said to have obtained a master's degree in public administration from the same university. Obtaining the two degrees is laudable, but the mystery is that not much is known about his completion of high school which is supposed to precede college education. This information remains elusive, since Weah dropped out of Wells Hairston High School in Monrovia to seek his path to stardom. This controversy fuels the integrity question that clouds his academic achievement.

When the news of Weah's educational attainment broke in Liberia, it was received with mixed reactions. Many pundits insisted that Weah had found the courage to go school because of his ambition to become president of Liberia. Many citizens, especially from the opposition, felt that Weah did not merit the degrees he obtained. They even denied that he had completed high school, because no information was available about the high school he attended. So the unanswered question is, How did he get admission into DeVry University? (Some even questioned the credibility of DeVry University.)

Meanwhile, Weah's academic achievements were the biggest news his followers ever heard prior to his election.

They were consumed by excitement and enthusiasm. They made a very big show of his return after his graduation. He had a heroic welcome fit for a rock star.

The party organized a very elaborate official ceremony for Weah to present his degrees to his supporters. They marched on the principal streets of Monrovia and hosted a lavished party at the headquarters of the Congress for Democratic Change (CDC) to honor the graduate, their standard-bearer, George Oppong Manneh Weah.

In essence, Weah's education from the day he tested the political waters in 2005 has been an issue of controversy. Weah himself is on record as admitting that he went back to school simply because he was criticized, saying, "Criticism made me go back to school."

Prior to becoming president, Weah was not known to have any major sustainable investment in Liberia. Unlike some of his soccer colleagues, who have great investments in youth development programs, education, and healthcare like Didier Drogba of Côte d'Ivoire, Mohammed Kallon of Sierra Leone, and Samuel Eto'o Fils of Cameroon, George Weah does not have tangible investments in Liberia. Between the late 1990s and early 2000s, he managed to organize a soccer club, named and styled the Junior Professionals, and opened a sports and recreation materials store named after himself. The soccer team was promising and even became the outstanding team in the country at the

time. The store was second to none. Understandably, after less than ten years of difficult operation, the two businesses collapsed due to poor management.

Weah also set up a small radio station named and styled Kings FM. The station was primarily a music station, which also promoted Weah with respect to his soccer accomplishments. The status of the station never befitted the character of a soccer icon of Weah's standing. Kings FM was housed in a cramped rented building and managed by volunteers who were predominantly apprentices in the field of journalism.

Indisputably, Weah remains the most decorated and outstanding soccer legend on the continent of Africa. He is recognized, honored, and respected as such. What even sets him apart from his generation of players is the fact that he is the only African player to have won the FIFA World and Europe Best. Obviously, Liberians are proud and well pleased with Weah's world soccer records. Definitely, in the soccer arena, he put Liberia in the spotlight internationally and his legacy as such remains an inspiration for his generation and others to come. Weah's soccer legacy is irrefutable.

On the other hand, despite these unparalleled accomplishments in stardom, his transition to politics, especially rising to the presidency of war-torn and impoverished Liberia, remains a mystery. It is true, as many

claim, that following the election of Madam Sirleaf in 2005, Liberia has taken another historic step by electing a soccer star president for the first time in Africa. Ultimately, the election of Weah, a celebrity with a peculiar background, is a story of interest considering the implications for the future of Liberia's fragile democracy.

There are serious concerns over his ineffectiveness as a politician as well as his strong links to former warlord and President Charles G. Taylor. The latter should not go unnoticed. Prior to the election, Weah earned the backing of defeated presidential candidate Prince Y. Johnson, who was aligned with Taylor during the early days of the bloody civil war, as well as being responsible for the gruesome murder of ex-President Samuel K. Doe. His party, the Congress for Democratic Change, formed an alliance with Taylor's National Patriotic Party. "They are our natural partner," Taylor's ex-wife and NPP Senator Jewel Howard Taylor was quoted as saying in November 2016. "The CDC was created out of the NPP and so the alliance with the CDC is a natural alliance."

News of the CDC and NPP partnership provoked mixed reactions from political pundits in Liberia and beyond. Some members of Taylor's party immediately suspended their membership, while several CDC partisans left because of the link with Mr. Taylor.

"The way Mr. Taylor ruled and tortured us during those days, I doubt anyone who suffered will ever forget those painful memories," noted entertainer Kekura Kamara, affectionately known as Balawala, who was a member of the Weah Public Relations team during his football playing days. "Weah is surrounded by Taylor's vampires. His former wife is his running mate; his security staff are all handmade by Taylor. You think he can control them? It's impossible."

"George was a very good footballer," Kamara said. "He showed that on the field but, as a politician, I doubt that he will make it." Kamara insisted that the CDC leader was a reactionary and deemed him an unpredictable decision maker. Having worked with Weah for several years, Kamara was sure that Weah's ideology could not be the same now as it was when he first launched his bid for the Liberian presidency back in 2005.

Interestingly, Weah's criticisms by several of his famous Lone Star teammates can be traced from the 2005 election to his second run in 2017, when they again refused to support him; some even actively campaigned against him. Speaking at a news conference on October 10 on behalf of several former teammates of Weah under the banner "Soccer Legends," former defender Dionysius Segbwe explained that their stance was "one of conscience devoid of any prejudice; it's a decision to support the strong foundation of President Ellen Johnson Sirleaf's administration." They also declared support for the former vice president, Joseph N. Boakai, emphasizing his competence, quality, and leadership ability to consolidate Liberia's democratic gains.

One of Liberia's celebrated football stars, James "Salinsa" Debah, who is also Weah's cousin strongly criticized Weah's decision to run for president in both 2005 and 2017. In a news conference also, Debah underscored that he was not supporting Weah because of the popular public inclination that he (Weah) was not educated. "My reason is that he does not have the necessary governmental experience. He is a novice who does not understand the intricacies of politics," noted Debah. The football star went on to say that as president, if Weah did not perform, everything he had earned in this world would be taken from him. Reacting to his cousin's criticism, Weah argued that Debah had no idea why he was running for president. "No one goes to the presidency with the requisite experience except they served before," Weah noted.

Debah's claim that Weah's lack of the necessary governance experience confirmed the obvious: that Weah possesses no corporate or political leadership experience. So the reaction provided by Weah is far-fetched. The truth is that you do not have to serve as president to gain experience before going back to serve. This reasoning is illogical. To be president, one has to possess a certain degree of leadership skills and values either in the corporate or government setting. The fact is that Weah had no experience outside of the soccer pitch, thus making him unfit for the presidency.

It is not uncommon that Weah rose to fame simply on account of his soccer iconic standing. His natural skills and talents for soccer, however, do not substitute for corporate or political leadership achievement. Hence, drawing from these deficiencies, as well as a flamboyant and extravagant lifestyle, the soccer icon may reasonably be expected to derail the gains that have been made over the years toward Liberia's postwar recovery, thus culminating in many years of setbacks. Another critical dimension has to do with the common view that Weah's election may become an inspiration for other stars on the continent of Africa to transition to politics by pursuing political leadership in their own countries.

Obviously, the continent should brace itself for this alluring political spectacle. Such a prospect is high and could be achieved at the expense of fame and popularity. This paradigm shift in African politics represents "blinking lights" alerting people to a serious menace to the growth of democracy in Liberia and eventually the entire continent. Thus, it is imperative to unravel the possible effects of an experimenting celebrity leadership in a struggling nation in transition, Liberia.

Chapter 4

The Incredible Voyage
to the Presidency

There was a semblance of hope in 2005 following the prolonged civil war when Liberia experienced for the first time the holding of democratic elections under the watch of the international community. The elections brought to power Africa's first female president, Madam Ellen Johnson Sirleaf.

Madam Sirleaf did not just rise to the country's highest office as an ordinary Liberian woman. She was a longstanding factor in the Liberian political arena and recognized globally for her stern fight against corrupt and brutal regimes and her boldness in speaking truth to power. Madam Sirleaf's profound understanding of global affairs and trusted relationship with influential Western capitals, especially Washington, propelled her over the years for her election in 2005 and 2011. She was an ideal candidate, and that's why she won those elections.

Although Madam Sirleaf won that historic election highly acclaimed nationally and internationally, that election era however witnessed the birth of a strange factor across the Liberian political spectrum. The participation of a celebrity, candidate George Oppong Manneh Weah, in the 2005 elections was a defining moment for our nascent democracy.

Despite Mr. Weah's defeat in a compelling runoff election, he won the hearts of a crucial segment of voters, the young people who were driven to love him naturally simply on account of his iconic standing. Then as now, the youth constitute the majority of voters in the country but sadly lack a basic understanding of the importance of making the right choices. Obviously, this has implications for the growth of Liberia's fragile democracy.

The moment Mr. Weah tested the political waters in 2005; it became clear that the days ahead on the country's political landscape would remain unsettled because of the "Weah factor." The reason is simple. He is a soccer icon without any trace of success in corporate or political leadership. Hence, assuming the highest office of the land needed the highest attention.

With such solid determination demonstrated by Mr. Weah, it beggared comprehension that political leaders could not visualize this factor as a historic groundbreaking moment for a disquieting shift in the body politic of

Liberia. These so-called political leaders in their persistent deception and hypocrisy have never been able to consult and forge genuine ideological alliances to strengthen and raise the bar of the political culture of the nation to reflect any standards or sanity. Consequently, the failure of the so-called political architecture to selflessly prevent this strange phenomenon from happening has further compounded the country's leadership dilemma.

Nonetheless, Madam Sirleaf's election represented hope that reassured many Liberians that the foundation of a shattered nation, a dysfunctional country as it was, without strong structures or systems in place, could be reestablished. The country was completely isolated and rendered a failed state when she assumed leadership. Mindful of her election also as a test to women's leadership in Africa and by extension, globally, Madam Sirleaf wasted no time in playing to the tune of the international community. By acting vigorously to organize an effective government with an acceptable structure, she demonstrated her commitment to uphold the rule of law. The president's rapid move to embrace democracy and embrace its tenets of fair play, equality, and justice placed Liberia under the international spotlight and set the stage for improving its image in the global community.

In particular, the establishment of integrity institutions such the Liberia Anti-Corruption Commission, the

Governance Commission, the National Elections Commission, the Civil Service Agency, the Liberia Revenue Authority, and the General Auditing Commission, consistent with her 2006 inaugural declaration to fight corruption as "public enemy number one," was a great prospect that further improved the country's image and considerably restored citizenry's trust and confidence in the government. The plain fact is that the successes achieved by the Sirleaf government during her first term were on account of these concrete actions.

Down the road in 2011, Madam Sirleaf succeeded herself for a second term after winning a second democratic election. This time, Mr. Weah was also on the ballot but as vice presidential candidate to Ambassador Winston Tubman, the presidential candidate. Mr. Weah also lost that election because many of his supporters lost faith in the ticket with Ambassador Tubman as standard-bearer. In effect, many of Weah's supporters were disappointed that Tubman did not represent the change they craved, eventually considering the Tubman-Weah ticket as a dilution of their revolution.

Another fact that led to Weah's defeat was the much-publicized speculation that he was using his run as a popularity stunt to extort money from some of his competitors, including candidates Ellen Johnson Sirleaf of the Unity Party, Counselor Charles Walker Brumskine of the Liberty Party, and his own standard-bearer, Ambassador Winston Tubman.

Too often, there were unconfirmed reports from credible sources that Mr. Weah was seriously involved in commercial politics, to the disadvantage of his party officials. This in my opinion fomented serious internal conflicts, which left several of his confidants disenchanted. All that soon became history as Madam Sirleaf benefitted from the spoils of this breakdown. She won the election and had the opportunity once more to sustain the transformation of the broken country she inherited.

By then, the government enjoyed tremendous international support, which triggered investment in various sectors of the economy. Prospects were encouraging. Revenue increased sharply. As a result, the national budget ceiling moved from $80 million (US) when President Sirleaf took over in 2006 to $600 million in 2018 when she left power. Through foreign direct investment, her government was said to have mobilized $16 billion to be put into the economy.

The attraction of such unprecedented investment can be credited to the professed commitment of the government to fighting corruption, debt cancellation, freedom of speech, promotion of gender equity, and protection of human rights, which rapidly transitioned the country from war to peace. The successful conduct of the two successive democratic elections of 2005 and 2011 went far to set the stage for democratic governance in Liberia in the aftermath of many years of bad leadership and economic stagnation.

Despite these great recovery accomplishments, Madam Sirleaf undermined her own legacy, to the disbelief of Liberians. She appointed her children and other family members to key positions in government. She appointed her sons Robert Sirleaf as board chairman of the National Oil Company of Liberia and Fumba Sirleaf as director of the National Security Agency. Her two brothers, Ambullah Johnson and Varney Sirleaf, served as minister of internal affairs at two different periods. The president's brother-in-law, Estrada Bernard, was also her legal advisor. President Sirleaf also appointed other confidants in key positions of trust.

These family members and cronies remained untouchable. The president failed to muster the courage to prosecute several government officials, including some of the same relatives and cronies, accused of embezzling millions in state resources as detailed in audit reports. These actions and inactions on the part of the president, particularly the lack of political will to deal with these creeping vices, seriously weakened her own anti-corruption campaign and eventually eroded her legacy.

Inevitably, it became obvious that by the time she left power, corruption had become pervasive, as seen by widespread fraud, bribery, and impunity which swamped her government and imposed serious economic hardship on the citizenry. Public officials enjoyed a free ride, clearly shown by their dishonesty and insincerity in managing the country and its resources. The latter part of Madam Sirleaf's presidency reflected gross mismanagement, endangering earlier gains and casting uncertainty over the future of the country.

Madam Sirleaf's departure from office was certain as provided for by law following two uninterrupted presidential terms (2005–2011 and 2011–2017). The president's exit was greeted by economic hardship. Life by then was extremely difficult, and her government turned out to be very unpopular, despite the huge international recognition. The writing was on the wall, and change was inevitable. Madam Sirleaf had to go.

The opposition Congress for Democratic Change (CDC), which strongly opposed the Governing Unity Party (UP) for twelve years, got reinvigorated and adapted a do-or-die posture in their quest to win the historic 2017 legislative and presidential elections. They were very optimistic, with soccer icon George Oppong Manneh Weah at the top of the ticket as presidential candidate and Jewel Howard-Taylor, the wife of former warlord and President Charles G. Taylor, as vice presidential candidate. In spite of the popularity of Mr. Weah and the support of Madam Taylor's party, the

National Patriotic Party (NPP) of former President Taylor, they were very mindful of the participation of the former vice president of Liberia, Mr. Joseph Nyuma Boakai.

Mr. Boakai, a statesman with impeccable leadership credentials, was in the spotlight. He was a committed and dedicated public servant and a distinguished diplomat with many years of service in both public and private sectors as well as an agriculturalist, educationalist, and outstanding administrator. Although Mr. Boakai served as vice president in the detested Sirleaf administration, he commanded a great deal of respect from the citizenry for his deep sense of humility and honesty.

With Mr. Boakai's unmatched reputation, education, and experience, it was obvious that he would become Mr. Weah's main competitor in the 2017 elections to replace Madam Sirleaf. Besides, many pundits averred that he was best situated to take over from Madam Sirleaf to consolidate the gains and surmount the economic challenges that beset the country. The elections of 2017 were crucial and considered as a benchmark for measuring the growth of Liberia's embryonic democracy.

Like the last three postwar elections, Liberians were visibly divided along two lines—the intellectuals and the common people. The CDC campaign, largely comprised of the youngest generation of voters, the unemployed, and the unskilled labor force, charged Mr. Boakai and his supporters, who were predominantly of the educated and working class, as being responsible for the bad state of the country's economy. They were inclined to believe that educated people had failed the nation. Thus, by inference, good leadership is not measured by the leader's level of education or experience. This was even conspicuously demonstrated by the CDC's official campaign song title, "The Country Giant," and the popular slogan of their campaign: "You know book, you don't know book, we will vote for you."

In addition, the CDC judged Mr. Boakai guilty by association for his role as vice president in the Sirleaf administration without objective evidence. Of course, their irrational inclination resonated very well with the CDC base, thus making their case even stronger. The urgency for change away from the Sirleaf leadership drove their campaign without any reflection on the obvious question, How would a CDC government govern differently from the UP government? Thus, the CDC and its candidates did not present coherent and implementable plans to the Liberian people as the platform upon which they sought to lead the country. Instead, they simply ran and got elected on mere slogans such as "That's our time," "Hope is alive," and "Change for hope."

Danger was lurking, but sadly, clueless voters had yet to come to terms with the impending reality. In essence, the focus of the campaign was primarily about change of leadership, not policy and strategy. So a clueless government was in the making. Like the celebrity Trump of the United States, celebrity Weah's quest was not about change in policy and strategy to effect growth and development. Rather, it was about becoming president to replace a predecessor.

On the other hand, the Boakai campaign, which was considered the camp of intellectuals and the working class, instituted a formal campaign structure and elaborated a comprehensive platform that was made public during its campaign activities nationwide. The Unity Party platform was well articulated at campaign rallies and debates, emphasizing the need for robust recovery. The plan prioritized construction of roads as a way of opening up the country to development in all spheres, investment in education, and health care, among others. Copies were adequately distributed nationwide with the aim of committing the party to addressing the economic and development needs of the country. It resonated well with the intellectual base.

This approach, however, walked right into a trap. Across the nation, segments of the population were already hostile to any form of intellectualism, since team Boakai was accused of failing the state. Intellectualism in the context of "book people" was rejected outright. Adding insult to injury was the widespread speculation that President Sirleaf had lent her support to the CDC. Even though she denied this on several occasions when asked by journalists, almost all her confidants defected from her party to the CDC without any resistance from her, apparently confirming the accusation.

Meanwhile, the conspicuous roles of her son Robert Sirleaf and Amara M. Konneh, the former minister of finance and development planning, as bankrollers of the CDC campaign were vivid manifestations in this regard. Historically, payment of West African Examination Council (WAEC) fees for junior and senior secondary school students has never been a standard practice of the government. Interestingly, during the 2017 exams right on the margins of elections, the government of President Sirleaf strangely announced that it was unable to pay the WEAC fees of thousands of students—something it had never done before. The fees have always been paid by parents without any issues. Little did the public suspect that the move was a ploy to boost the presidential campaign of Weah.

Following the announcement by the ministry of education, Weah's CDC announced that it would pay the WEAC fees of the students. In no time, students from affected schools flooded the CDC headquarters to receive their WEAC fees on a daily basis. The support of President Sirleaf even became clearer when candidate Weah informed the students that the CDC had run out of funds and was waiting for the president to replenish them.

This news went wide, and Madam Sirleaf's support to Weah's campaign was a secret. Even though the Weah campaign committed to the payment of the fees during the election, the remaining payment was done after the election by President Weah. Madam Sirleaf was never separated from the Weah campaign. She supported it in all aspects.

As the election approach, Madam Sirleaf artificially soured relations with her vice president as a means of staying away from all of his campaign activities. She went on record with excuses for not attending his campaign rallies. Notably, she stayed away from his official campaign launch in Monrovia after being informed officially. The president publicly acknowledged the invitation, and via the media, she said that she had a prior engagement to attend the dedication of a newly constructed clinic in one of the leeward counties. Absolutely no other occasion would have shown the president's lack of support to her vice president more clearly than her absence from his official campaign launch. That moment stamped her disapproval of the vice president's bid and her lack of support to him.

It was widely believed that Madam Sirleaf actually undermined the presidential bid of her longtime friend and vice president, Mr. Joseph Nyuma Boakai. Many well-meaning Liberians and the world at large could not fathom the depth of ingratitude exhibited by President Sirleaf toward a man who served her government and the

Liberian people with demonstrated sincerity, commitment, and dedication during her entire twelve years of leadership. Madam Sirleaf refused to identify herself with the Boakai campaign and was never seen at any of his major rallies.

The president made no contribution whatsoever to the presidential bid of the standard-bearer of her own party, the Unity Party. Strangely, it was no secret that she bankrolled the CDC campaign through her son Robert Sirleaf and the former minister of finance and development planning, Amara Konneh. Interestingly, Mr. Sirleaf may be blamed for having siphoned millions from the National Oil Company of Liberia for which his mother, the president, personally took responsibility. Sadly, she has yet to tell the Liberian people how and when she and her son will refund the stolen millions.

Remarkably, the liaison between Robert Sirleaf and Mr. Weah goes as far back as the special senatorial election of 2014. Mr. Sirleaf was desperate to win the Montserrado County seat in the Liberian Senate. This campaign began Messrs. Sirleaf and Weah deceptive relationship. The plan was for Weah, Robert's opponent, to surrender to Robert so that he would be elected and then reciprocate by supporting the presidential bid of Weah in 2017.

However, the deal failed because it became widely known that Weah had received money from Robert in exchange for his. Weah ran and got elected on account of his popularity. Absolutely, Weah's role as senator from Montserrado County from 2014 to 2017 did not record any concrete contributions through either debates on critical national issues, introduction or support to bills, or projects in his constituency (Montserrado County) within the framework of his oversight responsibility. Electing Weah to the presidency of an already wearied nation was a classy way of compounding Liberia's political and economic instability.

In spite of the fact that the process was plagued with grave unresolved electoral questions of fraud and malpractice, Mr. George Oppong Manneh Weah was declared president in keeping with the wishes of Madam Sirleaf and her cronies. The voters' roll that was used to ensure accountability in the voting process was riddled with flaws. Thousands of voters' names were omitted, some duplicated, and one voter identification number assigned to many other registered voters.

Ballots for the runoff election scheduled for November 2017 were printed in October after the first round. Immediately following the postponement of the runoff election to December, the ballots were distributed to the fifteen counties and remained there in the custody of the very National Elections Commission (NEC) that was reportedly in collusion with Madam Sirleaf and the CDC until December 26, 2017, for the said runoff election.

The prolonged entrusting of the ballots to the two political parties in the runoff, the CDC and UP, without any information regarding acceptable security measures reflected the gross lack of transparency and accountability that attended the electoral process. Sadly, all of those antidemocratic actions demonstrated by the NEC were dictated by Madam Sirleaf.

Her involvement in the 2017 electoral process to ensure a Weah victory was so extensive that when her fellow West African leaders assembled in Monrovia on the eve of the elections, the Guinean president, Professor Alpha Condé, did not mince his words. This is how he cautioned his Liberian colleague: "Please stay above the fray." In no uncertain terms, Professor Condé was bold and direct to Madam Sirleaf. Imagine if the president of a country struggling to come up to speed with the progress that was made in the consolidation Liberia's nascent democracy—just imagine if that president had to come to your country to upbraid you on your misdealing.

Madam Sirleaf's intention was clear. She needed to satisfy her side of the bargain with Weah, no matter what. Her family's security was more important than that of the state. Of course, she needed to hand the presidency to Weah because he primarily vowed to shield her and her family from legal action. Besides, he had to reciprocate her costly support to his election at the expense of her vice president and the future of the party that had handed her the presidency for two terms.

President Sirleaf and the National Elections Commission, under the watch of her appointee, Mr. Jerome George Korkoya, had no fear or concerns about the implications of their manipulations and maneuverings but pressed on to simply deliver highly questionable elections.

Once Mr. Weah assured Madam Sirleaf of protecting her no matter what, she did everything possible to ensure that he was elected, ignoring the impending adversity. Madam Sirleaf is a crafty woman who used her craft to lure Liberians into making her president.

The former president's sheer deception and ingratitude to Liberia was perfectly displayed when she betrayed her own committed vice president by assuring him of her support but then abandoned his presidential bid and fully supported the candidacy of Mr. Weah. She's also on record for planting a seed of discord in her own party (the Unity Party) for which the party expelled her. It is no surprise that the government of Mr. Weah is an offspring of Madam Sirleaf's evil desire. Today, the former president is haunted by her misdeeds, which rendered the 2017 elections controversial. The magnitude of the election dispute almost degenerated into a full-scale conflict.

In short, Mr. Weah was elected through a process entangled in serious controversies, but the decency and patriotic nature of the "declared loser" by the National Elections Commission, the Unity Party candidate, Ambassador Boakai, and his supporters gave peace a chance. It is safe to say that had it not been for the magnanimity of Ambassador Boakai and the opposition, the hullabaloo created by the NEC would have led to violent conflict during the 2017 elections.

Chapter 5

The Looming Danger

The presidency of any nation is the highest and most respected office of the land, and the one who occupies it is the symbol of the citizens. That's the extent of the importance of the presidency. A president has the core responsibilities of being the head of government, meaning the chief executive, vested by the constitution to conduct the affairs of the country. This requires the enforcement and execution of the laws. The president is the commander in chief of the army or military and oversees national security. As chief diplomat, the president conducts the foreign policy of the country.

In essence, to be president of a country requires a lot in terms of knowledge and leadership experience either in the corporate or political world. A president must possess a massive amount of know-how in order to do the job successfully. As president, one must have the clout to steer the affairs of one's country, navigating complicated domestic and international issues.

Apart from the core functions, a president should have the integrity and temperament to illuminate oppressed souls, resuscitate despairing hearts, energize the weary, rekindle hope in times of hopelessness, engender a sense of renewal, and unite in diversity. A president must rise above tribalism and ethnicity and look beyond race, creed, or alignments. A president should be a symbol of possibilities.

Conversely, Liberia elected a celebrity president in 2017 to replace Madam Ellen Johnson Sirleaf, following the end of her two successive terms. Electing a football icon, George Oppong Manneh Weah, who has at best limited traces of credible leadership experience, puts Liberia's recovery and development drive at risk. This likelihood is based on the fact that Weah was only elected on account of his football iconic standing. Weah has a questionable educational background. He is financially undisciplined, evidenced by his extravagant lifestyle with no meaningful investment in Liberia prior to becoming president. President Weah has a very short attention span and poor communication skills, especially when it comes to public speaking.

Like well-known populists—President Donald Trump of the United States; Britain's Labor leader, Jeremy Corbyn; and Rodrigo Duterte of the Philippines—Weah has introduced populism within the Liberian political spectrum. His emergence in Liberia's body politic is certainly an inspiration to the celebrity community to aspire for political leadership. In a struggling society with a history of profound economic perils, Liberia's fragile democracy is further threatened.

Liberia is one of the world's poorest countries with a poverty rate of 54 percent (World Bank, 2016). More than half of the country's population (4.614 million, as of 2016) is illiterate, with females accounting for the highest proportion. In 2007, the overall adult literacy of Liberia stood at 42.9 percent—among males 60.8 percent; among females 27 percent (UNESCO Liberia). In 2015, there was an improvement of nearly five points to an overall literacy rate of 47.6 percent (World Data Atlas).

Prior to the 2017 elections, the World Bank also reported that from 2014 to 2016, Liberia was bankrolled by huge foreign aid, suggesting that the country is one of the most aid-dependent countries in the world. The Bank recognized this as a problem and pointed out that the country's chief exports, iron ore and rubber, are in slumps, making them unattractive means of generating revenue.

According to the Bank, 50 percent of the country's gross national income was bankrolled by huge foreign aid flows, which may be put at risk with the election of Weah as president. With the closure of several aid programs prior to the elections, it became quite understandable that a

Weah leadership would be incapable of maintaining and consolidating the flow of aid, thus worsening the economic hardship in the country.

Liberia faces severe challenges of poverty and underdevelopment. The Bank also maintained that one out of ten households has electricity, and two-thirds of Liberians live below the poverty line. This preelection analysis suggests extreme impoverishment of Liberia, indicating the need for leadership with the know-how to institute the necessary short-, medium-, and long-term plans and programs to revive the crashing economy and keep it on a stable trajectory.

To the contrary, the country now has a president whose leadership is proving grossly incompetent and who lacks the integrity and capacity to deliver. Weah's government has yet to derive a comprehensive and workable development plan to fix the broken nation. There is no defined policy or strategy in place after six months in power to support any of the so-called development pronouncements of the government, signifying that the country has no genuine sense of direction under the Weah leadership.

There is no history of any government succeeding in economic recovery and development without a feasible plan and strategy. The fact that President Weah's CDC was in active opposition for twelve consecutive years and assumed the mantle of authority without any suitable plan speaks to the unpreparedness of the president and his government to lead.

This incapacity should surprise no one because during the elections, Weah evaded every engagement forum, such as debates or town hall meetings, with citizens who sought to evaluate candidates as to their leadership experience and plans to govern if elected. Weah intentionally stayed away from all of those crucial evaluation measures. He simply took comfort in his popularity as a guarantee for his election.

The president is now faced with the reality of navigating the colossal challenge of improving the country's fragile democracy, revitalizing the crashing economy, and restoring the broken infrastructure, education, and health care systems. This is an enormous task that seems impossible for a president who is new to governance.

As a consequence, in less than six months of Weah's leadership, the country is on the brink of economic collapse. The cost of living is very high, with households finding it extremely difficult to access basic necessities of life such as shelter, food, and clothing. Sadly, the government has not shown any sign of improving the worsening situation. Basic social services such as education, health care, employment creation and electricity are rapidly becoming inaccessible due to lack of appropriate policy and programs—in other words, government action.

The cost of building materials as well as the nation's staple food, rice, have sharply increased. Rice is a serious "political commodity" that triggers political destabilization in Liberia for decades, so it is incomprehensible that the Weah leadership has yet to initiate a viable investment scheme that seeks self-sufficiency in rice production.

The Rice Riot of April 14, 1979, which caused several deaths and the destruction of property, has always been a classy reminder. President Tolbert was assassinated in the immediate aftermath of the Rice Riot signifying the crucial role of the commodity in Liberia's body politic. Since that riot, rice continues to be a dominant factor that sways voters in elections. Almost every home in Liberia lives on rice, and any government that exhibits insensitivity to this historical fact always pays a price. With this historical backdrop, the government needs to immediately reform its approach to the acquisition, distribution, and sale of rice in order to make it affordable. This move should be considered a matter of urgency, given the significance of the commodity to Liberia.

Ironically, rice remains one of the most expensive commodities in Liberia. In fact, it has gotten worse since Weah assumed the presidency, with the price skyrocketing. The reason is simple. The president lacks vision, as does his government. Unsurprisingly, the importation and distribution of rice remains outsourced to a cartel known as Rice Importers of Liberia. The cartel for obvious reasons decides the quality and quantity of rice to be imported and distributed and the price at which it should be sold. In a feeble move, on February 1, 2018, President Weah convened a meeting with the five-member rice cartel, comprising four foreigners and one Liberian. The president urged them to reduce the price of rice in the meeting as though adding and subtracting numbers in black and white directly affects the price of a bag of rice in the store. Cluelessly, President Weah proposed a US$2.00 reduction in the price of the 25-kilogram bag and US$4.00 for the 50-kilogram bag. Of course, the rice cartel accepted the proposals but afterward refused to apply the reductions as proposed by the president.

Strangely, there has been no punitive action and no reengagement by the president with the rice importers for their nonadherence. It is highly probable that like his predecessors, President Weah has already been compromised by the importers in the first quarter of the first year of his leadership. Since the president's February meeting, the price of rice remains enormously high, with no indications of change on the horizon.

In the first place, it is not prudent to restrict the importation of rice to predominantly foreigners who are simply interested in colluding with the government as a whole or some elements within to maximize profit and rob the citizenry of millions. The poor majority dependent solely on rice has always been the victim of this robbery in broad daylight. The first intervention of any serious government in a precarious economic matter of this nature would be to open the importation of rice to all potential business entities guided by established policy.

In addition, the government will have to subsidize importation for a specified period to effectively lower the price of the nation's staple food. The second action is to invest significantly in rice production so that the country becomes self-sufficient and possibly even export rice to neighboring countries as a way of generating more revenue. Conversely, President Weah's approach was simply a deception, reminiscent of a star with no real impact on the high price of rice. This is a bad omen in view of the historical consequences when rice becomes unaffordable in Liberia.

A critical aspect of this problem is the uncontrollable exchange rate, which reflects a significant devaluation of the country's currency; the Liberian dollar. The exchange rate has reached a record high since the end of the civil war in 2003. The current exchange rate is US$1 to LRD$162. The country is currently facing sharp increases in gasoline and fuel oil prices. One gallon of gasoline is sold for LRD$540, while a gallon of fuel oil is sold for LRD$650. A shortage of these essential supplies on the market thus leading to the unprecedented increase in their prices is a recipe for tension and instability. It has direct impact on people's movement, livelihood, and commerce. Delays in making these supplies accessible and affordable has always proven counterproductive. Consequently, transportation fares have increased, many commercial vehicles are parked, many average Liberians traverse long distances on foot, and some private vehicle owners have also parked their vehicles due to their inability to purchase gasoline or fuel at such prices.

Furthermore, with the inadequacy of electricity supply, many businesses are using generators for their electricity, but the current price of fuel oil in particular is having serious adverse effects on their businesses. The drama is that commercial drivers cannot cope with the gasoline and fuel prices, and commuters cannot cope with the high transportation fares.

At the same time, production firms have increased the prices of their products such as plastic materials, toiletries, and assorted drinks. Since the exchange rate remains high, the prices of commodities are also high. Frozen storage and transport operators, in response to their rising costs, have raised the prices of their services and of frozen items where necessary. Overall, the living conditions in already poverty-stricken Liberia have gone from bad to worse.

Liberia is at the mercy of arbitrary forces when a celebrity president makes illogical decisions in flagrant disrespect of the laws. Instead of the president pursuing an immediate robust strategy to deal with the economic predicament, he has embarked on a disjointed and impossible line of development. Within months of assuming the presidency, without any baseline or feasibility reports, Weah promised to build a new Monrovia at Bali Island, construct a military hospital to be named and styled the 14 Military Hospital (his favorite jersey number), construct a coastal highway, and transform the slum community of West Point into a housing estate. The president's promises are impracticable.

In a country that is largely dependent on aid and without attractive borrowing strength, it is absurd to make such ambitious promises. Besides, the key policy questions of how and why remain unanswered, suggesting that Weah and his cohorts are treading dangerously. Such "planning" is completely illogical and doesn't reflect a development approach of the twenty-first century. Mere pronouncements do not get the job done. For a start, the presidency has simply demonstrated ineptitude of the highest order.

Undeniably, to embark on just one of those promises announced by President Weah, the basics must first be laid out: the legal framework should be in place, there must be a resource guarantee, the geography of the location should be appropriate, and the implementation plan must be developed to ensure the professional execution of the project.

Besides, the magnitude of each of the promises does not allow for them to be implemented simultaneously, the way they were conceived and announced. Liberia lacks the ability to generate the finances needed for such projects. No responsible government would make such rash promises in the face of the severe economic hardship facing the people. In the immediate term, concrete economic actions have to be taken to stabilize the exchange rate and reduce the prices of basic commodities, including major food items, building materials, and fuel and gasoline. Short-term jobs must be created, particularly for young people to help them address some of their basic needs, while developing sustainable medium-and long-term policies and strategies.

The sad reality is that President Weah is not only insensitive to these growing economic perils but frankly unable to address them. Pursuing his invisible agenda, President Weah has embarked on a private borrowing spree as an approach to fixing the country's problems. The president and his team of controversial economic advisors immediately consummated loan agreements with two private financing companies: Eton Financial Private Limited, said to be based in Singapore, and the EBOMAF Road Construction Company of President Weah's good friend, Mahamadou Boukoungou of Burkina Faso. The Eton Finance loan was $536 million; EBOMAF's, $420 million.

According to the president, the two loan deals were intended to construct 830 kilometers of paved roads as part of the estimated 3.4 billion–dollar cost of constructing roads throughout the country. The EBOMAF loan would cover the pavement of 323.7 kilometers of roads including the Somalia Drive via Kesselley Boulevard to Sinkor in Monrovia; 16 km from Tappita in Nimba to Zwedru in Grand Gedeh; and from Toe Town in Grand Gedeh County to the Côte d'Ivoire border, 10.2 km. It includes the 185 km road from Zwedru in Grand Gedeh County to Greenville in Sinoe County.

The Eton loan would cover 505.3 km of roads, including the 316 km corridor from Grand Bassa County in Buchanan through Cestos City in Rivercess County to Greenville City in Sinoe County and onward to Barclayville City in Grand Kru County.

Obviously, Liberia needs roads, especially since after a century and half, 94 percent or 11,000 km of roads remain unpaved. Although paving 830 km would be a drop in the ocean, it signifies a great step toward opening up the country to expand social services.

However, the unfortunate reality is that the Weah-led government did not demonstrate any sincerity in undertaking such needed investment. The loans were horridly and dubiously concluded, with serious implications for Liberia's already failing economy. Many financial experts described the unusual move by the government in pursuing private borrowing and the crafty way it was carried out as being entangled in treachery, bribery, and gross violation of the laws.

In the Eton Finance $536 million loan deal, the Weah government, without going through any competitive procurement process as required by the Public Procurement and Concession Commission (PPCC) Act, selected a subsidiary of Eton Finance, MAEIL Construction Liberia Ltd, as the "contractor," with the liberty to subcontract Liberian construction companies, without any competitive procurement process. The other problem here is that by being a subsidiary of the loan giver, Eton, MAEIL Construction will also be the loan recipient because it will be the one to whom the loan proceeds will go to finance the construction costs. Thus, aside from the flagrant violation of the procurement laws of Liberia, the Eton deal is problematic because of the potential conflict of interest inherent in having the loan giver serving as the loan recipient. In this circumstance, the incentive for hiking the cost of construction works in order to unfairly recover the loan proceeds is very high.

Clearly, the Eton deal lacked transparency and proper vetting. On paper the lender presents itself as a Singapore-based financial company. Investigation by one of the leading media institutions of Liberia, *FrontPage Africa*, had previously established that several weeks before the Liberia Loan arrangement, Eton Finance Private Limited, on May 7, 2018, reapplied to the Accounting and Corporate Regulatory Authority (ACRA) to be reinstated under the same name and unique entity number, 200510984K, renaming the same shareholders and directors (receipt number ACRA180507174296).

Additionally, a query by *FrontPage Africa* of the Singaporean Business Registration Portal (www.bizfile.gov.sg) using the unique entity number, 200510984K, obtained from Eton Finance Private Limited shows that the company status is still listed as "Struck Off," raising more questions about the company's capability to raise the money forLiberia loan.

The other piece of the unwanted puzzle is the shady, even more troubling EBOMAF loan deal. In deliberate violation of the Code of Conduct for Public Officials by President Weah, the Burkinabe owner of EBOMAF, Mahamadou Bonkoungou, compromised the Liberian president by gifting him a private jet. When the president realized the courage and persistence of the critical voices, he erroneously averred that the gift had "no strings attached." Within the following week, President Weah sent another loan deal in the amount of $420 million to enable his Burkinabe friend's company undertake the road construction contracts. President Weah's selection of his friend's company openly and blatantly violated Liberian laws.

The brazenness of President Weah's breathtaking loan deals was further exposed by the executive board of the International Monetary Fund (IMF). In their report the directors emphasized that "future debt obligations should be undertaken transparently, limiting new debt to concessional terms, with effective implementation of infrastructure projects."

The entire loan enterprise by the Weah administration was characterized by dishonesty, with an ulterior motive to defraud the Liberian people of millions of dollars. Despite the swift ratification of the loans by the legislature and President Weah's signing them into law, questions lingered over the numerous red flags reflecting serious conflict of interest and clear violation of the country's laws (the Code of Conduct for Public Officials and the PPCC Act).

In their hapless reactions, President Weah and his posse of officials took pride in a display of arrogance and disrespect to label critics of their shady loan agreements. Three of his kitchen cabinet members (ministers of finance and development planning, of state for presidential affairs and information, and of cultural affairs and tourism) were on social media (Facebook) telling citizens to "shut up" with their fingers placed to their mouths. It is unusual for government officials of such standing to display that magnitude of insensitivity in the midst of growing uncertainties. This reflects insolence and completely irresponsible behavior.

Even more, the open intolerance and greed speaks to the emergence of another era of a Liberian leader playing to the same colonnade. From all indications, President Weah is proceeding wrongly, raising doubts about the possibility of recovery, let alone sustainable development.

It is often said that first impressions matter in anything one does. President Weah's first major move—to secure the Eton and EBOMAF loans for major development of the country—leaves a horrible impression. The deception, dishonesty, and flouting of the laws characterizing the two shady deals, valued at nearly $1 billion, reveal the weakness and incompetence of the president and his government to lead Liberia in these critical times. In fact, the statuses of the two loans have now become a mystery, even as the government is under increased pressure to acknowledge that it unfairly branded critics against the controversial loans as "enemies of the state."

The president's inner circle or kitchen cabinet is packed with individuals of the questionable character marring historical Liberian politics. Some have serious credibility issues, while others simply enjoy the confidence of the president but lack requisite experience and know-how, as he does, thus accounting for the controversial and erratic approach to governance. As such, the government is embroiled with integrity, credibility, and capacity deficit. A careful look into Weah's kitchen cabinet with respect to handling the Eton and EBOMAF deals makes this reality evident.

The minister of finance and development planning, Mr. Samuel D. Tweah, is in charge and responsible for formulating, institutionalizing, and administering economic development, fiscal, and tax policies for the promotion and efficient management of financial resources of the government. Mr. Tweah is said to be one of the brains behind both loans (Eton and EBOMAF). Regarding the Eton loan, the minister acknowledged that the government failed to conduct due diligence on Eton Financial Private Limited before signing a US$536 million loan agreement with them. With respect to the EBOMAF deal made with President Weah's Burkinabe businessman friend, Mr. Mahamadou Boukoungou, the minister failed to address or discuss the loan's status.

In acknowledging infirmities of the Eton deal in an interview with *FrontPage Africa* (2018), the minister averred:

> "There have been legitimate concerns about either the viability of Eton, the legitimacy of Eton—we've received all of those queries and we have conducted our due diligence and

we are still in the process of conducting our due diligence. Due diligence is not a one-off event—it is a sequence of things that you can do. So, coming out of all of these conversations will ensure that we are making progress. But the notion that Eton is off the table is not true. Eton Finance—the loan we enter with Eton is a highly concessional loan and as I told the partners yesterday (Wednesday), that loan is concessional and I don't think they have an objection to its concessionality."

Minister Tweah also acknowledged that the administration which had so far been reluctant to heed criticisms was finally taking into consideration the sticking points being raised. "One of the challenges, one of the things is that when we signed the HIPC agreement—we agreed that—I think it was signed in 1986 or so with debt waiver—that countries that waived their debts cannot take loans that will then be non-concessional meaning high-interest rates." The minister explained: "Interest on the Eton is 1.46 percent. So, under the World Bank rules, concessional rules, Eton is fine—in fact they believe it is too good to be true."

The Eton loan is the product of a web of controversies ranging from violation of the laws to evading standard benchmarks. Even the IMF and the World Bank strongly advised against borrowing above the country's budget ceiling. In addition to this caution, President Weah was seriously criticized for granting a $420 million loan to his businessman friend, Mr. Mahamadou Bonkoungou's road construction company, EBOMAF, whose planes the president used for official trips—a clear violation of the code of conduct and a conflict of interest.

The minister of justice and attorney general of the republic of Liberia is Counselor Frank Musa Deen. The minister is on record for strongly defending the loan, although he failed to put his signature to the Eton contract when it was signed in Hong Kong. This was not just a paradox but a clear indication that he may have had his reservations but was halfheartedly riding along. In fact, after the signing ceremony, Senator Sando Johnson of Bomi County, speaking to the media, raised concerns that the memorandum of understanding was not signed by the minister of justice, the chief legal adviser to the president. "Firstly, if you look at the agreement, I think the Minister of Justice did not sign it, the Ministry of Justice is the legal person in this country, why didn't he sign it? So, we have to look at all this thing and ask what's going on?"

Despite his expressed reservation by reason of his failure to sign, the justice minister later described the Eton deal as one of the best loan agreements the country has ever entered into. He called on critics to give the process a chance and stop interposing hurdles to the process. "Some people say the people don't have website; will the money be sent through the web?" he asked rhetorically.

Counselor Deen, speaking in his capacity as the attorney general, said he had read the loan financing agreement, and "its benefits surpass petty consolidation." "If you enact this agreement, it becomes law that will impact our economy. The agreement does not impose any particular company. The Ministry of Public Works will do the vetting," the attorney general declared. It is only fair to point out that as the chief legal adviser to the president, the Liberia's attorney general has a great deal of responsibility in this matter.

Mr. Mabutu Nyenpan is President Weah's minister of public works—probably the man cutting the shots right now. Minister Nyenpan is responsible for adequately administering the engineering component of the state in surveying, drafting, designing, construction, and supervision as well as for improving and maintaining, directly or by contract, all highways, bridges, roads, streets, airports, seaports, and other public infrastructure. He has been very vocal about the need for roads. When he appeared before the senate during his confirmation hearing, the former Sinoe County senator underscored the need for a radical approach to addressing the country's age-old problem of roads, which according to him has become a "national security threat and national emergency … to be addressed."

The minister argued that Liberia's annual budgetary allotment to roads connectivity was too meager to address the chronic problem of bad roads in the country. Making the case for the controversial loans to be signed, the minister found himself in a complicated quagmire, believing on the one hand that intervention by bilateral partners in the road sector was inadequate to substantively change the situation. "We cannot build our country by relying on handouts or by thinking small. As Liberians and as a government, which got elected on an 'agenda of change,' we cannot continue to do 'business as usual.' Our people have hopelessly waited for far too long."

According to Minister Nyenpan, the financing agreements presented a unique opportunity for Liberia to change the status quo. He encouraged the senate to support President Weah in his road construction endeavor, adding that it was the president's first and foremost reality. However, it is evident that at no time did candidate Weah lay special emphasis on road construction. In fact, from his twelve-year opposition period to this point of his presidency, he does not have a single plan, not to mention one that reflects road construction as a priority. Meanwhile, although it is true that Minister Nyenpan is said to be more involved in the technical aspects of both loan agreements, his voice does not carry any significant weight to make a major impact or game-changing play.

Many Liberians have complained persistently about the reemergence of Emmanuel Shaw II in the Weah administration. It strikes many well-meaning Liberians as incomprehensible that it does not bother the president by any measure. Shaw was finance minister of Liberia during the Samuel Kanyon Doe era and is also a close confidant of former President Charles Taylor. He stepped down from his position as a member of the board of directors of Lonestar Cell/MTN to accept a role as one of the lead financial advisers in President Weah's government.

Shaw spent most of his time in South Africa during the Liberian civil war. He is no stranger to controversy and is well known as a wheeler-dealer. Many believe he has been one of the major engines behind the controversial loan deals. Although there have been efforts by griots (hereditary bards, instrumentalists, and singers) and by some of Shaw's aides to distance him from the shaping of the deals, his reputation with the late President Doe and jailed former President Taylor has made it impossible for many to believe that he does not have a hand in both the Eton and EOMAF loans.

It is also been ventured that Mr. Shaw is not having it rosy within the president's inner circle. There is a complete manipulation to win the president's confidence. Finance Minister Tweah made a smart move in an effort to address the speculations, categorically rejecting local media reports that he and Mr. Shaw were at loggerheads due to the fact that Mr. Tweah has been leading most of the discussions regarding the negotiations of the deal with Eton Finance Private Limited. In an interview with the *Daily Observer* newspaper (2018) Minister Tweah completely dismissed the reports, terming them as false. "Shaw and I are on good terms and there's nothing suggesting that we have a conflict for which he intends calling for my resignation."

It is often said that whatever is done in the dark will always come to light. This adage is true, and many people can easily relate to it. You cannot fake the truth. Besides, Mr. Shaw has a reputation that speaks for itself. Thus, it is obvious that no amount of behind-the-scenes overtures can distance him from the consummation of the two horrible loans.

Mr. Charles Bright, formerly a general in Charles Taylor's NPP government, crash-landed in the Weah administration. Mr. Bright's stock fell as soon as the controversial letter elevating him to a cabinet-level position surfaced. The scope of his task was directly consistent with that of the president in several ways. There were major concerns as to whether the president had read the letter before signing it because of the wide latitude of functions spelled out in the letter. Mr. Bright became the subject of discussions across the country with some equating him to a prime minister.

Bright, who served as finance minister in the Taylor government and has been President Weah's economic adviser, was General John T. Richardson's principal deputy, remembered for taking over the Housing Bank in Monrovia in military uniform during the heyday of Mr. Taylor's National Patriotic Front of Liberia in the infamous civil war. This is the president's letter to Mr. Bright:

> I, George Manneh Weah, Sr. President of the Republic of Liberia, by virtue of the power in me vested, do hereby acknowledge that Hon. Charles R. G. Bright, my advisor for Economic Affairs, has the status of a Cabinet Minister, with full courtesies and benefits appertaining thereto and commission him as follows:
> To visit all Ministries and Autonomies Agencies, Government Commissions, Public Corporations and State-owned enterprises (wholly and or partially-owned) to obtain information and advise me on current policies, practices as it relates to the operations of the Entity in General, and its personnel in particular;

To be an Ex-Officio participant in all meetings at said Entities, Board or otherwise, regarding matters with an economic impact on revenue, expenditure, personnel and other assets;

To ensure, as practical as possible that personnel actions, employment salaries, other benefits, dismissals, retirement and work schedule are in keeping with approved government guidelines;

To Monitor, Generally, all activities of appointed officials and with written approval of the Minister of State for Presidential Affairs, utilize the expertise of other Liberians as resource personnel.

In accomplishment of the above responsibilities, all head of autonomous agencies of government, public corporations and state-owned enterprises are mandated to fully cooperate with my above-named advisor and provide him with any and all information, documents and support requested.

It was clear that drama would ensue in the aftermath of such a letter. In no time, it was gathered that the controversial letter was written by Messrs. Bright and Shaw; and they got the president to sign it without reading, as usual. Amid fears and pressure from the minister of state for presidential affairs, Mr. Nathaniel McGill, that Mr. Bright was about to usurp President Weah's functions to become the most powerful man in his government, the president moved faster to appropriately cage Mr. Bright.

This fallout has created friction between Bright and McGill. However, for other, personal reasons, Mr. Bright still enjoys some degree of acceptance in the presidency.

Archibald Bernard is the president's legal adviser and a longtime friend. He is influential in President Weah's priority squad and has been involved in interpreting the fine prints of both the Eton and EBOMAF loans. But like Bright and Shaw, Mr. Bernard is also said to be caught up in an inner circle fight with McGill for the president's attention. The controversial loans remain the source of their relation and also function in a bigger picture: to protect the president's interests by securing the loans. Otherwise, it is unlikely they will get along.

Even though Mr. Bernard did not publicly speak out about the loans—a wise practice for a legal aide—it is not however clear whether he is in favor. Still, with his long history with the president, he remains a trusted legal adviser.

Without doubt, Mr. Nathaniel McGill is the most powerful man in the president's cabinet. Minister McGill has a hand in almost every major deal or loan agreement involving the presidency. He has reportedly been at odds with both legal adviser Bernard and economic adviser Charles Bright. Like Bernard, McGill has been in attendance for both Eton and EBOMAF memorandum of understanding signings and also working behind the scenes.

Minister McGill has a regularly used defensive mechanism for the loans. He is one of those steadily calling out the opposition, the media, and critics to give the Weah administration the chance to perform and halt their criticisms. The minister's blanket call did not, however, quiet the determined opposition and other critical voices. The fruit of their persistent criticism of the Weah government to abandon the negotiation of the bad deals is reflected in the unpopularity of the deals and their attending failures.

Minister McGill took strong exception to Senator Sando Johnson's criticisms of the Eton loan agreement. "This is one of the best loan agreements the country ever had; the criticism by some people including Senator Johnson is unnecessary. We took the loan to build roads for our people. We cannot allow this country to remain like this on grounds that we don't want loan." He furthered that the Weah administration would not relent in engaging loan agreements with any financial institution globally.

Although Minister McGill's influence seems to be growing by the day, he may yet run into the Ellen Johnson-Sirleaf and Morris Saytumah experience during her first term.

Liberia is a peculiar place. Many things happen in Liberia that don't easily take place in other countries. There are three branches of government in Liberia; the legislature (the first branch), the executive, and the judiciary. They are separate but coordinate branches of government in keeping with Article 3 of the 1986 Constitution of Liberia. This is all becoming a matter of having the law but enforcement a matter of choice, as the president is tightening his grip on the legislature.

The leaders of both the senate and the lower house of the legislature have come under fire by the president of late for forming part of delegations with the executive branch to seek loans. Albert Chie, president pro-tempore of the senate in particular, oversaw the senate's speedy passage of both loans. President Weah got the process running early, taking both Chie and Speaker Bhofal Chambers of the House of Representatives on trips in hopes of cementing his grip on the legislature with the end game of a later smooth approval of the two controversial loans.

The senate under Chie passed the loans despite concerns about Eton's lack of credibility and financial history as well as conflicts of interest surrounding the EBOMAF deal and

President Weah's ties to the firm's leader. Additionally, the central issue regarding the Central Bank of Liberia— whether the government's consolidated account was being put on the line in order to secure the US$536 million loan from Eton—was completely ignored.

When Bhofal Chambers was elected speaker of the legislature's lower house, it was expected that one of the most vocal critics of former President Ellen Johnson Sirleaf would make a difference in shaking off the bad image of the legislative body. Seven months in, many political observers say, Chambers has been a major disappointment and embarrassment. Overseeing a body that approved two controversial loans with numerous red flags curbed the confidence many had in the once-robust lawmaker who was a thorn in the side of former President Sirleaf.

It was Chambers who sent the loans to the upper house following a 4-G passage for concurrence without conducting due diligence.

During his inauguration, Chambers promised to reform the lower house, declaring: "I will like to let you know that you will not be disappointed. This House will be rebranded. Your hopes will not be withered. We will build your prospects. I want to thank the President, Madam Ellen Johnson Sirleaf, as one who led this country, though there were challenges, gaps and weaknesses, we still understand that she did what she could."

It is dangerous that the deadlines for both loans have already elapsed but the two controversial loans still have the force of law. Although they have not been consummated into handbills, the silence from both houses of the legislature, which speedily passed the loans, remains a complete mystery.

So one can avow that in Liberia, President Weah risks treading the same path as his predecessor, Madam Sirleaf, who always protected those within her inner circle, in many cases to her own detriment. The delay and uncertainty over the loans from EBOMAF and Eton are reflective of a state of denial and silence, with both the executive and legislative branches of government unwilling to face the encroaching realities that pose serious complications to the fulfillment of the Weah administration's pro-poor agenda.

In the aftermath of the failure of the two shady loan deals, the World Bank made an offer of $500 million for road projects. The move by the World Bank is certainly well intentioned, to help the country solve the age-old problem of poor roads, which has hampered development in Liberia in almost every sphere. The World Bank is an outstanding global financial institution with a strong reputation for supporting development activities particularly in developing countries. In fact, the Bank has a long-standing history of development assistance to Liberia dating back to the 1960s through both financial and technical resources. Therefore, the $500 million offer to the Weah government is just part of the Bank's continuing efforts toward development in Africa.

However, the Bank is mindful of ensuring that Liberia meets established standards and necessary preconditions for the award of the loan. The process will require time as well as ensure adherence to basic regulations, fulfillment of guidelines for international competitive bidding, and completion of an economic or social rate of return analysis. This approach of due diligence ensures accountability that both protects the integrity of the World Bank and saves Liberia from financial predators. Besides, neither the Bank nor the government has a choice simply because no financial institution would choose to willingly dump their funds into a bottomless pit.

Notably, the loan in question is simply an offer, contrary to ongoing statements from the government that it has secured another loan from the World Bank pending the so-called Eton and EBOMAF loans. The fact is that the two loans were scams and have since perished. They were short-lived due to their controversial nature, particularly their load of far-fetched stipulations. There is no doubt that if officials of the government don't desist from their militancy and their irresponsible approach to governance and instead demonstrate a sense of responsible leadership, the country risks losing the World Bank's offer. It is the poor citizens who will again be victimized, since Weah and his cohorts are already living in splendor.

According to a Liberian public policy analyst, Mr. Boakai Jaleiba, a graduate of Georgetown University in the United States, the Bank will not lend to Liberia under the current status of the governance procedures. Mr. Jaleiba highlighted that there is no Public Procurement and Concession Commission attestation, no debt sustainability analysis, and no risk analysis to cover dynamic macroeconomic factors in the future. He added that at the current stage of negotiation, the World Bank has only volunteered to work with multilateral development banks such as AfDB, EBRD, EIB, and ADB to raise the money.

Another potential risk that looms in Liberia is the move by the Weah-led government to dip into the country's foreign exchange reserves for the payment of salaries and other services. Pundits have spelled out the dangers of a country tampering with its reserves in such a manner, warning that it may hurt the country's credibility and borrowing capacity.

In December 2005, the net reserve as reported by the Central Bank of Liberia (CBL) was $6.5 million. According to them, by December 2017, Liberia's gross international reserves position, including special drawing rights and reserve tranche, was at $517 million, reflecting significant growth.

During the last decade that preceded the 2017 elections, one of the foremost priorities of the government was building its foreign exchange reserves. Financial experts have underscored that a strong foreign exchange reserve position increases confidence of foreign investors and helps boost foreign direct investment. It also helps by stabilizing the local currency exchange rate. A strong reserve position further helps, as mentioned, by maintaining international credibility and improving financing capacity.

Of course, the World Bank offer is the third major loan facility President Weah is going after, barely six months into his leadership. He is hardly making progress, but quite astonishingly too, he's stuck into it. The president's loan spree has become a circumnavigating venture in which he gets to announce huge figures and receive lots of praise. That is exactly what celebrities enjoy doing—being glorified by griots heaping praises on their shadowy dictators such as President Weah out of hypocrisy and sycophancy.

It is common knowledge that President Weah's insecurity on the job reflects his lack of basic understanding of the presidency. Six months in office was enough to showcase his qualities and capabilities, and this he has done. He has demonstrated no vision for the country. He has failed to provide a sense of direction for the country. Many of the citizens are disappointed, particularly his diehard supporters, who feel left out of the equation. They now feel abandoned and are very disenchanted.

From the outset, the president urged them to lower their expectations. Doing so was almost impossible due to the solid assurances given them during the campaign. Harping on slogans like "That's our time" and "Hope is alive" was enough for anyone, especially adherents of the CDC doctrine, "With Weah, all things are possible" to have doubt that they were already employed. Indeed, the president and the entire CDC did not realize the implications of such indoctrination until the election was won and reality settled in.

There are hundreds of thousands of unskilled and unemployed young people in the streets with the illusion that Weah will perform a miracle to earn them jobs, turning some into business tycoons and creating fat bank accounts for others. So, in effect, they are actually keeping hope alive that their master, President Weah, will turn Liberia into a utopian society. It is dangerous that many misled Liberians, especially young people, view the president as a messiah and are still dreaming about the creation of an ideal world that is yet to come.

Even though the president in a nationwide address appealed to citizens to be patient amid the current economic hardship in the country, the expectations of his supporters remain extremely high. This has become a topical issue of national concern, as the young people involved are predominantly unemployed. Some lack skills and have engaged in drug abuse and crime as a means of survival. Others have skills but cannot get employment opportunities. They also resort to crime to earn a living.

If this trend continues unabated, social problems will persist. Communities will no longer be safe and secure. The growing tension in the country will scare away potential investors, thus undermining any development initiative. Interestingly, not even the so-called messiah, President Weah, will be spared from such menace because there is no way that a desperate group of people will lower their expectations and be patient indefinitely.

The call doesn't worth it. It is clearly time for the president to listen, learn, and lead, because he holds the key to hopes, dreams, and aspirations. Can this president cultivate the leadership skills of listening and learning in the middle of the game? Surely, he should, but the other question is whether he is even aware that he has to do so immediately. Here is why I believe he is not. The president has never benefited from such orientation. Besides, he is a celebrity with a strong inclination to pun and pageantry. The president likes informal social events in glamour where he can be fully in charge.

To put it plainly, listening, learning, and leading are not his line of business. He has a very short attention span, which makes it difficult for him to grasp and follow through on details. Additionally, as a celebrity politician the president has the charm to deceive by giving the wrong impression to his diehard supporters that he is the antidote for failure. That is the drama right now in Liberia. Much is going wrong, but shockingly, President Weah is still being worshipped.

Right next door in Sierra Leone, President Julius Madaa Bio is well on course with his development agenda. He has a plan that's guiding his development approach. He has instituted policy reforms leading to major changes that have situated his government to appropriately get into motion in less than two months. Key government institutions are being audited based on need, and those found culpable will be prosecuted as a way of addressing the culture of impunity and minimizing corruption.

The Sierra Leonean president, as part of his immediate or short-term plan, has also directed investment in sectors like health care, education, and youth development services in order to effect social change. In less than two months in office, President Madaa Bio has demonstrated responsible leadership and competence. At the end of his first hundred days, a comprehensive report was made to the Sierra Leone people highlighting the gains made, challenges encountered, and prospects for achieving recovery and development.

Conversely, President Weah has been in office for a period far longer than his counterpart, Madaa Bio who assumed office barely two months ago. The fact that Madaa Bio was able to achieve so much by establishing the foundation of his government in one month shows that Sierra Leone has good prospects for recovery and development.

By contrast, the absence of an acceptable working agenda to guide the governance process speaks to President Weah's poor leadership ability. Forging unity and harmony among the citizens is crucial since development thrives best in conditions of peace and harmony. There's a likelihood that achieving this milestone will prove futile, given the president's divisive statements and approach to Liberians who oppose his policies.

It beggars comprehension to hear the president, who is supposed to be the symbol of love, hope, and unity, referring to certain Liberians as "enemies of the state." This undemocratic move by the president is not strange because he's rapidly revealing his dictatorial tenets. Liberia's embryonic democracy is in jeopardy.

The president is also on record for threatening the BBC stringer in Liberia, Jonathan Paye-Layleh. At a well-attended joint press conference with UN Deputy Secretary General Amin Mohammed at the ministry of foreign affairs in Monrovia on March 22, 2018, in his response to a question from Mr. Paye-Layleh, President Weah bluntly declared, "You are one of those that were against me."

The president's outburst was by no means taken lightly, especially coming from the chief executive of the republic who controls the army and national security forces and conducts the foreign policy of the country. From such a position of strength, his attack on Paye-Layleh was considered an attack on the media, since media institutions and individual journalists were constantly being attacked similarly. Surrogates of Weah intensified the attack on Mr. Paye-Layleh to the point that he had to flee from the country to the United States, raising serious national and international concerns about the state of freedom of the press only months into Weah's leadership.

The president is also seeking to exercise his influence over the judicial branch of government, evidenced by his frantic efforts to impeach one of the justices, Counselor Kabineh Ja'neh. Justice Ja'neh wrote an elaborate and astute dissenting opinion in the elections fraud case, *National Elections Commission v. Liberty Party*. Justice Ja'neh opined that when a violation occurs and it is acknowledged or reported, it should be considered a violation. According to Justice Ja'neh, a violation as such doesn't change to something else.

Justice Ja'neh differed with his colleagues on their opinion in which they ruled in the landmark 2017 elections case that "there were instances of electoral irregularities and fraud but the magnitude of the irregularities and fraud were not sufficient to affect the overall conduct of the elections"—thus denying the Liberty Party of its claim that the elections were characterized by irregularities and fraud.

The reality was that Weah's CDC was in solidarity with the National Elections Commission because it had already situated the party (CDC) to win the election. Thus, President Weah did not want any form of obstruction or hindrance to his victory. Ruling against the NEC would have affected President Weah's chance of winning the presidency. In that case, Justice Ja'neh's dissenting opinion was counterproductive for the CDC. For the CDC, Justice Ja'neh is perceived as an opposition to them on the Supreme Court. Therefore, he should be removed.

In the president's campaign to remove Justice Ja'neh, representatives of the CDC in the House of Representatives have introduced a bill of impeachment in which they have fabricated accusations such as misconduct, abuse of office or power, fraud, and corruption.

Similarly, the president nominated a long-sitting senator, Counselor Joseph Nagbe, as associate justice to replace Justice Philip A. Banks III, who has retired from the Supreme Court. The nomination of Counselor Nagbe further disclosed President Weah's move to expand his influence and authority. The president, the House speaker, the president pro-tempore, and now Counselor Nagbe are from the southeastern region of the country. This is a deliberate attempt to significantly shift power to the southeast and strengthen the president's power base.

The appointment of Counselor Nagbe is also considered by pundits as a deliberate violation of Section 2.4 of the judiciary law of Liberia which provides that anyone nominated to the Supreme Court must be engaged in the active practice of law for at least seven years prior to his nomination. Second, the judiciary law of 1972 defines active practice as being in the judiciary, teaching at the law school, or being involved in litigation at the ministry of justice. Indeed, if the president meant by this appointment to strengthen the bench, guaranteeing professionalism and independence, he would have nominated legal luminaries who are not in short supply.

The nomination of a vibrant and practicing legal scholar like Counselor Nebalee Warner, dean of the Louis Arthur Grimes School of Law, who earned a master's degree in law, or Counselor Jallah Barbu, an expert in law with a law doctorate, to replace Counselor Banks would have demonstrated great leadership on the part of the president. Instead, he nominated a sitting senator who has been out of active practice for many years. Although the senator was a member of the judicial committee of the senate, that was not enough to make up for the missing litigation experience to qualify for such a crucial position when the country is struggling to transform the judicial system.

The ratification of the president's shady and failed loan agreements (Eton and EBOMAF) without any form of due diligence speaks to the extent of his influence over the first branch of government, the legislature. The action of the legislature to approve the two agreements at the president's pace bespeaks a total disregard for their obligation to check and balance as provided for by law.

The spirit and intent of those who crafted the constitution to have three separate but coordinate branches of government has been relegated to a dead letter and does not exist in practice under the Weah leadership. Without checks and balances, President Weah has been given a blank check. Shamelessly, the legislature again passed a resolution to give the president an unrestricted mandate to seek more loans. Playing to the gallery of the president with such subservience only confirms the firmness of his grip on the legislature.

Going after the three branches of government in order to exercise absolute control is a clear attempt to erode the underpinnings of democracy and replace them with totalitarianism. The actions of the president threaten to destroy the gains that have been made to create a democratic space with the tenets of fair play, equality, and justice. Allowing a novice like Weah to control the three branches of government is detrimental to the survival of democracy in Liberia.

President Weah claimed to be a man not just of words but of action. He made the assertion during his inaugural address on February 22, 2018, at the Samuel K. Doe Sports Complex. "My greatest contribution to this country may not lie in the eloquence of my speeches. But it will definitely lie in the quality of the decisions that I will make." The president promised the Liberian people to make not eloquent speeches but quality decisions. If the decisions made during his first six months as president are quality decisions, based on his reasoning, then Liberians urgently need to redefine *quality decision* moving forward.

Mr. President, blatantly violating the laws of Liberia is not a good decision. Negotiating bad loans is not a good decision. Characterizing your citizens who oppose your disastrous policies as "enemies of the state" is not a good decision. Attacking journalists is not a good decision. Failing to address the economic hardship facing your people is not a good decision. Not at all; Mr. President, these are not good decisions by any measure. Rather, good decisions solve problems, engender love, promote peace, and unite people irrespective of their race, culture, tradition, or affiliation. Regrettably, the president's version of good decisions is a recipe for many years of setbacks.

At least his predecessor had some minimum standards. Assistant ministers or equivalent were required to have bachelor's degree or above, deputy ministers or equivalent needed a master's degree or above, and ministers or agency heads needed a master's or PhD. The issue of experience was a subject of importance as well. These minimum standards played a significant role in instituting a professional-based government that transitioned Liberia from a failed state to one better recognized.

In spite of its economic paralysis, the governance apparatus has structures and systems that simply need to be strengthened and improved for effective governance. On the contrary, President Weah's government is swamped by mediocrity. There's no room for standards in his government. Standards and benchmarks put in place by his predecessor to ensure quality and productivity are rapidly being eroded by his freestyle leadership. Anybody, regardless of background, can serve in any position. Specialty or expertise really does not matter.

That is why many of Weah's officials are serving based on their loyalty to him or the CDC. The number of years one spent in the so-called twelve-year opposition struggle is an excellent basis for their appointment. Another point of entry in Weah's government is recommendation from his chief benefactor, Madam Sirleaf. Many of her top officials are currently serving in the Weah administration for that reason. They include Minister of Information, Cultural Affairs and Tourism Len Eugene Nagbe; Minister of Foreign Affairs Gbehzohngar Finley; Deputy Minister for Foreign Affairs Elias Shoniyin; and Minister of Internal Affairs Varney Sirleaf, her brother.

On a serious note, several senior officials like the ministers of state for presidential affairs and of finance and development planning, the press secretary to the president, and a host of deputies are for the first time serving in such high-profile positions, thus making it very difficult for the government to find a balance that will enable it to deliver. For example, the mayor of Monrovia City, Jefferson T. Koijee, is a university dropout. The assistant minister for research and extension service at the ministry of agriculture, Alvin C. Wesseh, was expelled from the University of Liberia for acts incompatible with his status during his undergraduate studies. Many of them have very limited or no experience at all in the areas where they have been called to serve.

So the government is overwhelmed by inexperienced and wholly incompetent people serving in key positions of trust. The difficult start of the government and early failures in its undertakings are anchored on this reality.

Also for this reason, it is not surprising that the government is operating without a plan. Once any of the kitchen cabinet members conceives an idea, he or she offers it for immediate attempt. In that case, the end justifies the means. That's why everything in the country is just occurring impulsively with no defined approach. Meanwhile, it is foolhardy for anyone to think that out of President Weah's limitations would come a productive leadership. The president is constantly appearing at groundbreakings and launch programs. Even some of the ongoing projects initiated by his predecessor, such as construction of roads and health and education facilities, are being relaunched and rededicated.

The president seems to have a huge taste for infrastructure development, but with the current fragmented development approach, it is far-fetched. In an eleven-page report compiled by the Center for Policy Action and Research (CePAR), on using an alternative model when looking at development, CePAR argued that overreliance on investing in hard infrastructure will not deliver the prosperity Liberia craves; rather, it is the investment in human capital development that will unleash the development potential of Liberia.

CePAR says the new evidence suggests that the difference between rich and poor countries from the development perspective can be largely explained in terms of their priority approach to human capital (education and health) rather than any other development indicator. Also, economic growth in countries with higher levels of education tend to be more sustainable and long-term, with markets showing greater resilience and dynamism when compared to countries with the lowest educational levels. The report asserts that economic growth in rich countries is based on investment in people (education and health), while growth in poor countries relies heavily on extraction industries and exploitation of mineral resources.

As with funding infrastructural projects, CePAR recommended that an alternative model of financing needs to be sought outside the budgetary allocation as a means of focusing on human capital development. A minute levy on personal income or petroleum for education is one plausible way to fund human development. Similar measures are being instituted in Côte d'Ivoire, Nigeria, Kenya, Tanzania, South Africa, and twenty-five other countries across the world, and the results are outstanding. CePAR's analysis of the importance of investing in human capital should form the basis for the development approach of President Weah's government because sustainable development is guaranteed by an informed and vibrant (educated and healthy) citizenry.

With an educated society, opportunities exist for new ideas (creativity and innovation), technological advancement, infrastructure development, employment creation, and economic growth. It goes without saying that no amount of infrastructure development survives in a predominantly illiterate society. Even in the present state of affairs, maintaining Liberia's poor infrastructure is almost impossible. The reason is simple. Most citizens lack the most basic understanding of those infrastructure systems and their strategic importance to development.

Unfortunately, President Weah's government development approach is not scientific (methodical, technical, logical, or systematic). It does not rely on development indicators. The government acts by instinct, reflective of unrealistic pronouncements and launches of undocumented development projects. To date, no one has an idea of the rationale for a new Monrovia when the current Monrovia has yet to meet minimum city standards; for construction of a military hospital when existing health facilities are yet to reach their full capacities; or for construction of coastal highways and transformation of an entire slum community without any guarantee of resource availability.

These mere pronouncements came at a critical period when the economy was collapsing, imposing extreme hardship on the citizenry. The move by the government to embark on these huge and long-term capital-intensive projects with no regard for the priority of dealing with the unbearable economic situation clearly manifested the lack of know-how to lead. Thus, it is a safe guess that chances are slim that the Weah government will invest in human capital development.

An essential dimension of Weah's governance in Liberia that remains amiss is its foreign relations approach. To begin with, Liberia's relation with the United States has strategic importance and cannot be treated as a secondary subject. The relationship has a long history deeply rooted in the birth of the nation as an offspring of the United States. The relationship has always been special, and whenever it has weakened, the aftermath has always proven counterproductive.

Circumstances surrounding the collapse of the regimes of Presidents Tolbert, Doe, and Taylor are classic examples of why strengthening or improving relations with the United States is vitally important. Madam Ellen Johnson Sirleaf understood it well and succeeded in commanding the respect and support she enjoyed not only from the United States but the international community as a whole. The importance of Liberia's relationship with the United States cannot be overemphasized.

Thus it is incomprehensible that President Weah's government has no clear approach to relations with the United States. Ever since the United States recognized Liberia as a sovereign nation fifteen years after the declaration of independence, the diplomatic trend has not changed and will not easily do so. The United States takes the lead in the provision of support to Liberia's development. The role of the United States in this respect is an encouragement or a green light for other nations, donors, and philanthropists to meaningfully engage with Liberia. Obviously, powerful

Western nations will adapt a "wait and see" approach, letting the United States take the lead before they follow.

Since President Weah took over the mantle of authority, he has been seen deeply involved with the French and some other European and Arab nations. As expected, those moves will only register the usual glamour associated with leaders' meeting, exchange of pleasantries, and according each other the courtesies required. Sometimes, there are unpacked agreements in the form of communiqués or memoranda of understanding that never easily get implemented. Seldom do such meetings or state visits result in practical donations, especially when there are implicit conditions such as the current situation with the United States. The truth is that these moves will only translate into meaningful support toward national recovery and development, especially genuine economic transformation, depending on the status of Liberia's relationship with the United States.

In March 2018, President Weah nominated Ms. Gurley Gibson as ambassador-designate of Liberia to the United States, Canada, and Mexico. Prior to her nomination, Ms. Gibson once served as first secretary and Foreign Service Officer (FSO) of the Trade and Investment Office in Philadelphia, Pennsylvania, in the United States. She managed the trade and investment office until resigning her post as FSO in 2013. Ms. Gibson's resignation came on the heels of President Sirleaf's activities in New York during the United Nations General

Assembly. The cause of Ms. Gibson's resignation was never disclosed, but it was preceded by a series of audits conducted at the trade and investment office.

Interestingly, almost five months after Ms. Gibson was nominated by President Weah as ambassador-designate, she had not been confirmed by the Liberian senate; nor had she taken over in Washington from Counselor Lois Lewis Brutus, the current ambassador. The conspicuous silence of the government as usual is a clear indication that something wrong is going on. However, Ms. Gibson's nomination did generate serious speculation that she had been rejected by the US government because she is an American citizen. The information became a major discussion topic across Liberia and on social media, particularly Facebook. In an attempt to rescue the situation, the government, through the ministry of foreign affairs, clarified that the rumors about the ambassador-designate's rejection by the US government were "unfounded lies." Refuting the claim further, the ministry of foreign affairs through its assistant minister for press and public affairs, Mr. Sylvester Pewu, reiterated that the information about the Ambassador-designate was a "blatant lie." "It is unfounded and the Ministry of Foreign Affairs has no such information about our Ambassador-designate being denied." These "clarifications" from the government did not stop the rumors that Ms. Gibson could not serve as a diplomat for Liberia.

One of the leading local newspapers, *FrontPage Africa*, contacted the United States embassy near Monrovia to speak on the issue, and Paul A. Hinshaw, the embassy's public affairs officer, underscored that the US government would not offer any comment. "The Embassy does not discuss questions of diplomatic nominations with any party other than the Ministry of Foreign Affairs."

If the United States did not reject Ms. Gibson, it is fair enough for the senate to confirm her. Otherwise, Ms. Gibson's nomination has to be withdrawn if she cannot be confirmed by the Liberian senate with reasons provided like the case of the then minister of justice designate, Counselor Charles Gibson. Counselor Gibson's nomination was withdrawn by the president in the aftermath of serious public outcry about his involvement in acts incompatible with the status of the office of the minister of justice.

On the contrary, Ms. Gibson's nomination has become a laissez-faire issue; something that doesn't speak well of President Weah's foreign policy; worse, dealing with the United States in such an uncertain manner significantly damages the government's credibility. At the least, this is a bad omen for Liberia–Unite States relations.

President Weah is on record as assuring the Liberian people he upholds the rule of law. In fact, the president read selected provisions from Chapter II (General Principles of the National Policy) of the Liberian Constitution (I,

e. 1986 Constitution) during his first State of the Nation address in a joint session of the legislature. He said: "What is expected of us, who have been elected by our people to govern them? What is really expected of those of us who have been entrusted with the responsibility to lead them? The answer is to be found in Chapter 2 of our Constitution, from which I shall now read selected articles extensively and verbatim." He went on to read from Articles 4 through 10, emphasizing that he would discharge his duties and functions in adherence to the laws of the land. The seven articles from which the president read represent the fundamental principles in the governance of the republic and serve as guidelines in the formulation of legislative, executive, and administrative directives and execution.

It seems the president's show of committing himself to upholding the rule of law was just for the span and glamour of the occasion. After less than a year of President Weah's leadership, there are creeping tendencies that ultimately pose a threat to the rule of law. The president continues to violate the very laws that he pledged to uphold. There are mounting concerns about the future of the dispensation of justice, press freedom, freedom of speech, and human rights.

The president blatantly violated the code of conduct for public officials in his attempt to grant his Burkinabe friend, Mahamadou Bonkoungou, a mouthwatering contract worth $420.8 million. Before the loan was submitted to the legislature for ratification, Mr. Bonkoungou was constrained to return the aircraft he claimed he had borrowed from President Weah. The two men insisted that there were absolutely no strings attached to the plane that was given to the president. Barely a week after their lies, President Weah submitted the shady $420 million loan agreement with his friend's company to the legislature for ratification.

Additionally, the president violated the PPCC Act by not subjecting a contract agreement of such magnitude to the procurement and concession laws of the country. Nor was the Eton loan process subjected to the PPCC framework as required by law.

At the nation's referral hospital, the John F. Kennedy Medical Center, President Weah appointed the administrators in breach of the established system. Candidates for administrator of the JFK are vetted by the Civil Service Agency (CSA), and then names are sent to the board for appointment. In the case of President Weah's first appointment, the regime was reversed. Similarly, at the National Transit Authority (NTA), the president usurped the functions of the board by directly appointing the entity's administrators.

President Weah is also on record for grossly violating Section 2.2 of the 2009 Act that established the Liberia Extractive Industries Transparency Initiative (LEITI) in March 2018 when he appointed one of his friends, Mr.

Gabriel Nyenkan, as executive director of the integrity institution. Prior to Mr. Nyenkan's illegal appointment, LEITI was headed by Mr. A. D. Konah Karmo, who was appointed by the Multi-Stakeholders Group (MSG) of LEITI in 2014 following a competitive recruitment process in which all stakeholders participated, in keeping with the law that created the entity.

The president's illegal action claimed the attention of the Extractive Industries Transparency Initiative (EITI), the global standard for the good governance of oil, gas, and mineral resources. The head of EITI's Global Secretariat intervened by engaging with the president, but that process proved futile, and Mr. Nyenkan has retained his position. Mr. Nyenkan's appointment was strongly condemned nationally and internationally, thereby calling into question the integrity of the president's decisions.

LEITI's Multi-Stakeholder Group has the statutory mandate to oversee LEITI. It is a tripartite conglomeration of the civil society, private sector companies, and the government, in accordance with Section 2.2 of the act that established it. The LEITI Act of 2009 requires the president to appoint members of the MSG and "designate one of them as the Chairperson and another as the Co-Chairperson."

"The power to recruit the Head of Secretariat, Deputy and other staff members of the LEITI Secretariat therefore lies with the MSG, according to Section 6.3d of the LEITI Act."

These illegal actions sharply contradict the president's commitment to upholding the Constitution. President Weah's arbitrary actions are worrisome and constitute a threat to the survival of the rule of law. His frequent outbursts and branding of opponents, particularly those who do not agree with his unpopular policies, are characteristic of a dictator. Calling members of the opposition community "enemies of the state" for their courage to hold his government accountable and angrily lashing out at the BBC stringer in Liberia, Jonathan Paye-Layleh—"You were one of those that were against me"—bespeak a lurking danger that must not be taken lightly. Coming from the president of the country, such behavior is cause for serious concern.

The CDC of President Weah ran on a dangerous doctrine, "That's our time" and "Hope is alive." These complementary slogans were never in any measured length. They were as loose as the CDC concept of change, which was to simply replace the Unity Party government with a CDC government. The change was never about policy or strategy that would point to how the CDC intended to govern differently from the UP. So hopes and expectations soared, and in the popular imagination Weah became a magic man with the might to change everything in Liberia. Obviously, the CDC train was unstoppable. The election was held, and oops, Weah became president, and it was certainly their time. So don't expect the people to remain hopeful, even though many do not have basic marketable or survival skills like carpentry, masonry, or plumbing. They must be employed by all means.

The pressure to provide jobs for hundreds of thousands of CDC partisans has constrained the leadership to set up a so-called vetting mechanism at CDC headquarters to recruit and deploy partisans across government ministries and agencies. It has now become a practice for various entities to deploy a certain number of partisans whose names, proposed positions, and contact details are forwarded to the heads of ministries and agencies in a special letter by the CDC chairman, Mr. Mulbah Morlu.

Failure to implement the chairman's mandate by any given entity in question is not a choice as it amounts to defiance, and only the chairman knows the nature and magnitude of the consequence. The positions of authorities in the various entities are threatened. This strange employment bonanza for partisans of the CDC began with the submission of twenty-eight names to the Liberia Water and Sewer Corporation (LWSC). The CDC chairman's list comprised seventeen recommended consultants, a monitoring manager, transportation manager, deputy transport manager, finance manager, cost accountant, administrative accountant, logistics manager, commercial manager, monitoring and evaluation manager, procurement analyst, and finance manager.

The hiring of the twenty-eight CDC partisans created a floodgate for government to absorb hundreds of CDC partisans. The National Transit Authority (NTA) was next in line to land over thirty members of the CDC. Similarly, at the National Port Authority (NPA) which is the gateway to the country's economy, the acting managing director, Celia Cuffy-Brown, is on record for rejecting fifty young men and women from the CDC who stormed the NPA headquarters in February 2018 following Weah's ascent to the presidency.

Ironically, Madam Cuffy-Brown hired three of the president's brothers to serve in three positions she created, signaling nepotism—a practice for which the CDC strongly criticized the then governing Unity Party. Prince Weah serves as Public Relations Strategist and makes a gross salary of $4,500, as do Walla Weah as Local Authority Liaison Officer and Moses Weah as an evaluation officer. The action of Madam Cuffy-Brown to hire the Weah brothers in the way she did is a strong indication of the Weah administration being entrenched in nepotism and corruption. The silence of the president on this matter speaks volumes. Not only is it a clear manifestation that he sanctioned the action; it also sends the message that he has fallen prey to corruption.

Several other government ministries and agencies are under pressure to consider a litany of names from the ruling party, including the Liberia Airport Authority, Liberia Maritime Authority, National Social Security and Welfare Corporation (NASCORP), and Liberia Civil Aviation Authority. This unsuitable and arbitrary practice has the potential to further impose strains on the already crippled economy by padding the payrolls of ministries and agencies, resulting in an upward shift in the wage bill. The other dimension of this danger is that for sure, "Their time has come," signifying an urgency. Understandably, partisans of the CDC cannot be told to wait indefinitely because they were assured of paradise, and it has come. Dangerous perception, isn't it?

The "power of fame" at most times demands blind loyalty. In the eyes of his loyalists, "Weah is divine," meaning he is faultless. In his kingdom, there can be no objectivity, no independence, and no criticism. Love Weah, respect Weah, and honor Weah. In fact, worship Weah.

This utopian belief has generated utter disrespect and arrogance on the part of Weah's supporters toward the "critical minds." So anything that is not "Weah-like" is an enemy. This is a dangerous mind-set that's taking serious roots in Liberia. The consequence of such a doctrine can be disastrous. The regime of President William V. S. Tubman, the military regime of President Samuel K. Doe, and the reign of Warlord/President Charles G. Taylor are good examples of such dangers.

With these creeping vices, it is no doubt that Liberia risks becoming a dictator's paradise where the governing apparatus will be saturated with gossips, lies, and betrayals. The Public Relation (PR) system of the William V. S. Tubman era may return, and people will live but in silence. Insecurity will set in, giving rise to suspensions, stage-managed coups, incarcerations, and secret killings. Character will no longer matter, and lives will be exacted in payment.

Integrity institutions may lose their force and simply exist, not in practice but on paper, creating a floodgate for greed, dishonesty, and corruption to take charge, subjecting everyone in order to prevail. The already falling economy will further bleed, and hardship will grow and set in. Depending on what action is taken to salvage the situation and how soon, chaos might find relevance, and poverty, illiteracy, and disease will continue to flourish.

My intent is not to cast doom but to unearth the dangers that are rapidly emerging. The indicators of what is to come are visible and have been properly discussed in this book. So it is prudent to underscore that mediocrity has taken over Liberia with the election of a football star, George Oppong Manneh Weah, whose background is completely unrelated to the functions of the presidency.

People are growing ever more impatient, and there's gross insensitivity not by choice but by the highly incompetent leadership of President Weah. This is evinced by the continuous demonstrated ineptness of the government to institute plans, especially immediate or short-term plans that would situate the government appropriately for the six-year journey to rekindle the hope of the people.

The government keeps crediting itself for countless groundbreaking ceremonies for the commencement of road construction projects, the adrift military hospital, housing estates, a pointless new Monrovia, and so on. These highly publicized projects have yet to take any meaningful shape or form, because they were founded on lies and deceit without a single plan. None complies with established legal frameworks. Thus, just as these awkward action had no guarantee for securing needed resources, their future is as bleak as that of the government itself.

Moreover, President Weah now takes pleasure in the dedication of ongoing projects of his predecessor, Madam Sirleaf, with his surrogates spinning everything to justify that the credit belongs to the president. Meanwhile they claim that the Unity Party government of President Sirleaf achieved nothing of magnitude, a completely meaningless assertion.

The point is that even if the CDC-led government of President Weah never had plans in place for her twelve-year opposition period, there are several pro-poor or recovery and development policies from which the party can derive an acceptable pro-poor agenda. Following several months of criticism from the opposition and pundits about the government's unprecedented and incoherent development approach, the ministry of finance and development planning is now grappling with the reality of developing a plan.

The simple fact is that if such a plan doesn't resonate with the hopes and aspirations of the people in terms of land ownership, it will become merely shelf material. Eventually, the erratic or acting-by-instinct governance model will continue. This fiasco, however, doesn't come as a surprise because of the dearth of ability that has beset the Weah government.

The irony is that as heavy-handed as President Tubman was, he had a development approach popularly known as the "open door policy." Although the plan had its shortcomings, such as very limited control measures for potential investors, Tubman's government had a sense of direction. His successor, President Tolbert, instituted the famous "from mat to mattress or Higher Height" policy, still considered one of the most promising policies for success in transforming the economy to better the lives of citizens, had he lived to fulfill his full presidential term.

Despite his autocratic rule, President Doe also had a development-oriented mind. He was extensively investing in infrastructure development. In particular, he adopted a strategy to construct buildings that would house government ministries and agencies in order to save the government millions of dollars that it paid to private building owners for housing government agencies.

That undertaking saw the construction of the new defense ministry in Congo Town, which was demolished by the Sirleaf administration to construct the ministerial complex. The current ministry of health in Congo Town, the huge Liberia Broadcasting System building in Paynesville, and Samuel Kanyon Doe Sports Complex are among the government's own buildings credited to President Doe's regime. Additionally, President Doe instituted the "green revolution" policy to invest in agriculture, in hopes of making Liberia self-sufficient in food production.

In his infamous state as president of Liberia, Charles Taylor instituted a national policy, "vision 2024," as his government's agenda to deliver the mandate of the people. Even with his erratic leadership style, Mr. Taylor had a plan by which he would be held accountable.

When Madam Sirleaf took over a completely dysfunctional nation, her government adopted plans in different stages, with the aim of situating the country appropriately for national recovery and development. The first inclusive plan, developed during her first term from a nationwide consulation, was the Poverty Reduction

Strategy Papers (PRSP). The PRSP was later transformed into the Poverty Reduction Strategy (PRS). The policy was very inclusive and reflected the development needs of the people because needs and strategies articulated in the plan were directly recommended by citizens during months of countrywide baseline survey.

Having made significant progress toward instituting structures and systems, the government was fully operational following a decade and a half of anarchy. The administration next instituted a very long-term sustainable growth agenda named Agenda for Transformation (AFT). The AFT was the vehicle for Liberia Rising 2030 Vision. Madam Sirleaf's approach established a legacy of restoring a completely shattered nation by forming a government where no structure, systems, and resources existed on the basis of deploying the requisite human and material resources, implementable policies, and strategies. Although she undermined this legacy by conceding to corruption and nepotism, President Sirleaf had plans that worked.

A critical dimension that represents real danger is President Weah's persistent violation of the laws of Liberia (i.e., the Code of Conduct for Public Officials, the PPCC Act, and statutes that govern agencies of government). The intolerance of his government towards the opposition and continuous threats to advocates of resistance (critical voices) signify the emergence of tyranny. These are clear signals that Liberia is at a crossroads; strongly suggesting that concrete actions have to be taken to make sure that democracy is unconditionally protected to guarantee the rule of law, freedom of the press, freedom of speech, and protection of human rights. If President Weah is to continue in his role as president of Liberia, he must be made to govern within the confines of the laws. Liberia cannot afford to slip from the path of democratic governance in any shape or form.

His initial arbitrary actions as president have made it abundantly clear that President Weah is running counter to the commitment he made to the Liberian people during his inaugural ceremony and first state of the nation address in January and February 2018, respectively, that he would govern within the parameters of the law. Liberians are rapidly losing hope in what he made them believe, that his leadership would be the antidote for the age-old chronic disease of corruption and impunity. This belief strongly informed the decision of many of his supporters to vote him to the country's highest office.

Another indication of leading on a dangerous premise is President Weah's approach to dealing with corruption, a scourge that largely accounts for the backward state of Liberia. The president's ludicrous assertion that everyone in Liberia is related, and so he will not be able to fight corruption, is the weakest excuse of a Liberian president for refusing to confront what may be Liberia's worst enemy. This statement represents the degree of the president's weakness and incompetence to lead. Above all, it echoes that he is equally corrupt.

By this statement, the president has given his officials the sturdiest incentive to go ahead and recklessly loot the resources of an already poor and war-ravaged nation. The scars of the war are yet very visible, evidenced by the broken economy, the poverty-stricken population, and poor social services and infrastructure. For many, electing President Weah was their hope for restoring the economy and giving meaning to their lives. On the contrary, they have been assured by their president that the journey to economic viability, peace, and stability cannot yet begin.

It is likely that President Weah's government may not cooperate with calls for the establishment of a war and economic crimes court (WECC) in Liberia. Establishing the court would facilitate implementing the recommendations of the Truth and Reconciliation Commission (TRC). The comprehensive recommendations consist of five essential components: (1) Accountability: Prosecution Mechanism, (2) National "Palava Hut" Forum, (3) Amnesty, (4) Persons Not Recommended for Prosecution, and (5) Reparations. The full implementation of the TRC recommendations would effectively contribute to dispensing justice, addressing crucial unanswered reconciliation questions, and setting the stage to end impunity.

In essence, the implementation of these recommendations is paramount to achieving genuine reconciliation. recovery, and development. The establishment of the WECC is consistent with the TRC framework, which calls for the prosecution of individuals, armed groups and other entities that the TRC determined were responsible for "egregious" domestic crimes, "gross" violations of human rights, and "serious" humanitarian law violations.

The failure of Madam Sirleaf's government to muster the will for the establishment of the court and subsequent prosecution of alleged perpetrators has made genuine reconciliation almost impossible in Liberia. Today, while many victims of the war are languishing unattended, their perpetrators remain scot-free. Several of them are living in luxury overseas from the spoils of the war; others arrogantly prowl the corridors of power in their various capacities as authorities of the nation.

This is an urgency that calls for immediate attention because the horrible experiences of the war are still fresh in memory due to the prolonged absence of genuine reconciliation. Even former President Ellen Johnson Sirleaf, after twelve years of her leadership, admitted to her government's failure in doing much to reconcile Liberians and subsequently deal with the scourge of corruption. In her last state of the nation address, former President Sirleaf cited corruption and reconciliation as challenges of her government.

Madam Sirleaf's steps to initiate the Palava Hut dialogue program was just part of her efforts to evade the prosecution involved in implementing the TRC's recommendation. Understandably, that would amount to suicide. In fact, not much attention was ever given to the so-called palaver-hut dialogue because those conversations did not in any way address the real issues of torture, rape, killings, and looting of the economy.

The United Nations will have to act through its Security Council by sanctioning the war and economic crimes court for Liberia and ensuring that President Weah's government cooperates, since that did not happen during the regime of his predecessor. Liberia is part of the global community and a member of the United Nations. The intervention of the United Nations and other world and regional bodies is much needed to assist Liberia at this critical juncture. The establishment of the court is crucial to achieving genuine reconciliation and addressing the problem of impunity in Liberia.

However, it is unlikely that the government of President Weah will demonstrate the political will to embrace and support the establishment of the war and economic crimes court in Liberia for several reasons. First, Mr. Weah was appointed as Peace Ambassador of Liberia, but establishing the war and economic crimes court was never a part of his agenda. He has never mentioned the need for decisively addressing impunity in Liberia in any of his statements as UNICEF Goodwill Ambassador, Peace Ambassador of Liberia, and now as president for the last seven months.

A second important indication that President Weah lacks interest in establishing a WECC in Liberia is his express commitment to shield Madam Sirleaf from prosecution. It is understandable that it is consistent with that comment for the president not to accept the war and economic crimes court, which would prosecute the former president in accordance with the TRC's recommendations.

During candidate Weah's campaign for the presidency, he failed to criticize Madam Sirleaf in any serious way, as a major opposition candidate would do. Instead, he graciously graded her at 80 percent for her performance as president of Liberia, an absurdity which created serious contradiction in his quest to replace her. Weah's protection of the former president is nonnegotiable. Even in the face of her admission of having made financial contributions to the infamous National Patriotic Front of Liberia of Mr. Charles Taylor to support the brutal civil war, and the mountain of accusations presented by audit reports and international antigraft institutions that she used her government to siphon millions from Liberia, President Weah's protection of the former president remains unshakable.

Similarly, President Weah is committed to protect Senator Prince Y. Johnson, former warlord and head of the defunct Independent National Patriotic Front of Liberia (INPFL). Senator Johnson strongly supported the presidential bid of then candidate Weah. The senator aggressively campaigned for him and encouraged his own kinsmen from his county, Nimba, to vote for Weah. It is clear that Weah will not embrace the war and economic crimes court because that would mean allowing the prosecution of Senator Johnson, one of his allies. Senator Johnson is infamous for murdering the late President Samuel K. Doe and many Liberians during Liberia's civil war. Senator Johnson would definitely be in the queue for prosecution by the court if established in keeping with the TRC's recommendations.

It is no secret that reform in Liberia is fundamentally important for strengthening and improving governance. However, it is increasingly clear that the Weah government may balk at reforming the 1986 Constitution. The government has yet to demonstrate any commitment to upholding the rule of law, which should be a determining factor for comprehensive law reform in the country. Only when the laws are appropriate and adequate are we able to improve and strengthen governance in the country.

Unfortunately, as soon as President Weah assumed power, his first move was to attempt to initiate granting citizenship and the right to own land in Liberia to non-negro descendants. As it stands, the Constitution of Liberia prohibits such rights. Citizenship and land rights–related issues were serious debates prior to President Weah's ascent to office. Instead of making time to set the stage for his leadership journey, since his government had no such plans, the president ignorantly raised a song when he had no idea about its meaning.

According to the president, doing so will accelerate development, improve the economy, and create jobs. The president's move was seriously criticized by Liberians at home and in the diaspora, stressing that first he needed to transform the crashing economy he inherited and carry out comprehensive reforms with emphasis on the laws which would situate the country appropriately for such a delicate conversation. Many argued that issues such as land and citizenship are crucial and thus should be treated as a long-term plan with priority given to short-and medium-term plans to revitalize the harsh economy and alleviate the hardship presently facing the country.

The 1986 Constitution, the organic law of Liberia, was drafted and adopted during the regime of the military junta, the People's Redemption Council (PRC) of Head of State Master Sergeant Samuel K. Doe. Many provisions of the

1986 Constitution are now either archaic or ambiguous and therefore not easily applicable in the current dispensation. The 1986 Constitution is the source of the culture of imperial presidency because it gives the president all but unlimited power as evidenced by Articles 54 through 61. Power is centered around the president not by choice but by the dictates of the Constitution, thus accounting for the centralized nature of the government and authoritarian rule.

Several other provisions of the Constitution are subject to review because of the problems associated with their application or enforcement. The provisions of chapter IV on citizenship, chapter VI on the executive, chapter VIII on political parties and elections, and chapter X on autonomous public commissions all need to be revised and expanded with the aim of addressing current reality.

Granted, there were attempts by the Sirleaf administration to amend certain provisions of the Constitution, but based on the magnitude of the problems associated with the 1986 Constitution, it requires thorough revision or else the drafting and adoption of a new Constitution which will meet the hopes and aspirations of the people. But again, with the laissez-faire attitude of the Weah administration, the prospect of reforming the 1986 Constitution remains unlikely.

From all indications, in President Weah's Liberia, there is growing uncertainty about entertaining merit, honesty, and accountability. There is no guarantee that these ideals will have a place in the present dispensation. That is exactly why citizens should now muster the courage to ensure that President Weah governs within the confines of the laws. This is fundamentally required for consolidating the gains that have been made in creating the tenets of fair play, equality, and justice. Citizens should hold President Weah's government accountable to these nonnegotiable standards, no matter what.

President Weah's concession to corruption further reflects the biggest scandal in the history of Liberia, the reported disappearance of $16 billion (Liberian), the equivalent of US$104 million. The money was said to have been printed by the Sirleaf government and brought into the country via the Roberts International Airport (RIA) and the Freeport of Monrovia. The RIA is the country's main airport, and the Freeport is the leading seaport and gateway to the country's economy.

The missing $16 billion represents 5 percent of Liberia's GDP, which when applied appropriately by the government could meaningfully address some of the pressing basic social issues such as health care, education, and roads. The money disappeared without a word from the Sirleaf government about authorization and printing of such a volume of Liberian dollar banknotes. Similarly, there was no word from the Weah government about circumstances surrounding the money's delivery, its clearance from the two ports of entry, and its subsequent application in the economy until the information was leaked by the Liberian media.

As the news broke, President Weah's government was drawn into a disjointed media blaze with senior government officials spewing lies, contradictions, and controversies. The approach by government in dealing with the scandal was completely irresponsible. The government's communications machinery broke down, brewing fear and tension in the country. Citizens remained confused and did not know whom to trust in President Weah's government.

The minister of information, cultural affairs and tourism, Mr. Eugene Nagbe, who also served in the same capacity in the Sirleaf administration, informed the Liberian people that the monies were printed in three different countries— Lebanon, China, and Sweden—and that several Economic Management Team meetings were held with the Central Bank of Liberia (CBL) on the matter. For his part, the former executive governor of the Central Bank of Liberia, Mr. Milton Weeks, who also held on to his position for some months into the Weah leadership, claimed that the money was only printed in one country, Sweden, thus contradicting his colleague, the information minister with whom he served in the Sirleaf government.

In like vein, the minister of justice and attorney general of Liberia, Counselor Frank Musa Deen, confirmed in an official ministry press release that investigation into the missing container with $16 billion was underway. The press release indicated that the money had been coming into the country from November 2017 to August 2018 through the RIA and the Freeport of Monrovia. This information from the minister of justice confirmed that the Sirleaf government had had the Liberian banknotes printed and that they were delivered into the country and received in the early stages of the Weah government. Paradoxically, the minister's press release underscored that the government of Liberia (Weah's government) was not informed.

The Weah government moved dramatically to identify and declare fifteen employees of the CBL as persons of interest to assist with the investigation and subsequently barred them from traveling out of the country. Ironically, no employees of key agencies of interest to the investigation were deemed persons of interest, including people connected to the Freeport of Monrovia, RIA, the Liberia National Police (LNP), the ministry of finance and development planning, and the legislature. The decision of the government to deliberately remain silent on the role of employees of all these suspicious agencies reflects the lack of credibility in the investigation process.

Through another press release the government announced the expansion of the so-called investigation committee to include youth groups, the religious community, civil society organizations, the International Monitory Fund (IMF), the Federal Bureau of Investigation (FBI), and the United States Treasury Department. The government, however, failed to inform the people as to whether or not it had written and received confirmation from the FBI, IMF, and US treasury department. Obviously, these are credible institutions whose consent to participate in an investigation of this nature requires a process. So it became clear that those organizations would not be moved by an ordinary press release or a phone call, as demonstrated by the government through the ministry of justice. A serious government would definitely consummate an understanding with such institutions before releasing information to the public.

Another aspect of concern with respect to the so-called investigation had to do with the rationale for including the IMF, civil society organizations, religious groups, and youth groups in a criminal investigation. Criminal investigation is very unique and delicate, requiring seasoned professionals and field workers. Thus the inclusion of non-criminal justice–related institutions did reflect an ulterior motive geared toward seeking empathy and influencing the outcome of the investigation.

Interestingly, on September 20, 2018, the minister of finance and development planning, Mr. Samuel Tweah, declared that no money was missing, thus dismissing claims by the ministers of justice and information and the former Central Bank governor. The following day, Minister Tweah again told Reuters that not all of the money in question was missing, thus contradicting both his colleagues and himself.

The president did not demonstrate leadership in calming citizens and giving them hope of a speedy investigation and outcome. The inconsistencies and incoherence in the government's approach clearly indicate that the scandalous situation is out of control. Their responses or reactions to this shameful and embarrassing scandal proved that President Weah's government is dishonest and immature and lacks the credibility to lead. The approach of the government in handling the scandal is erratic and has caused more confusing and harm than answers.

Anxiety and apprehension are rampant in the country, especially where expectations are high, and resentment has been growing due to the rapid deterioration of the economy since Mr. Weah took office. President Weah and his benefactor, former President Sirleaf, are the chief culprits in the mysterious disappearance of $16 billion, but most likely they will find scapegoats so that both of them can go Scott-free. However, times have changed, and the court of public opinion is not kind to President Weah and his predecessor. From all indications, the $16 billion scandal is a defining moment for the Weah presidency. No matter how it is resolved, the scandal is a bad omen.

Citizens should consider their role in standing up to President Weah's misrule as a matter of right under the laws of Liberia. They must demand from the government unconditional respect and protection of the rule of law, guarantees of press freedom and freedom of speech, and the protection of human rights. Citizens should adopt a pragmatic approach in keeping the president's feet to the fire to demonstrate accountability and transparency in the management of the country's resources. Otherwise, the democratic efforts exerted over the last decade will become meaningless, and Liberia will continue to slide backward.

Bibliography

Library of Congress. (n.d.). 1820 to 1847: From Colony to Republic. Retrieved from https://www. loc.gov/collections/maps-of-liberia-1830-to-1870/ articles-and-essays/history-of-liberia/1820-to-1847/

Fred P. M. Van Der Kraaij. (n.d.). President Samuel K. Doe (1980-1990) The Master Sergeant President. Retrieved from http://www.liberiapastandpresent.org/ SamuelKDoe.htm

Comfort Ero. (Sept 25, 1995). ECOWAS and the sub regional peace keeping in Liberia. *The Journal of Humanitarian Assistance.* Retrieved from https://sites.tufts.edu/jha/ archives/66

International Monetary Fund. (2007). Liberia: Interim Poverty Reduction Strategy Paper. Retrieved from https:// www.imf.org/external/pubs/ft/scr/2007/cr0760.pdf

Webmaster Adim. (Dec. 16 2013). The 5 Poorest Countries in the World. *Liberian Observer.* Retrieved from https://www.liberianobserver.com/business/the-5- poorest-countries-in-the-world/

Biography.com Editors. (April 2, 2014). Pete Seeger Biography. *A & E Television Network.* Retrieved from https://www.biography.com/people/pete-seeger-9542618

Ibrahim Al-bakri Nyei. (23 Oct 2015). Moving toward Constitutional Reform in Liberia: How legitimate is the process? *African Centre for the Constructive Of Resolutions of Disputes* (ACCORD). Retrieved from https://www.accord.org.za/conflict-trends/moving-toward-constitutional-reform-in-liberia/

Atty. Mohammed E. Fahnbulleh. (Sept. 21 2016). Fighting corruption In Liberia: Historical trail and accommodation. *Capitol Times.* Retrieved from http://www.capitoltimesonline.com/index.php/editorial/op-ed/item/1393-fighting-corruption-in-liberia-historical-trail-and-accommodation

Economic Community of West African States (ECOWAS). (2016). History. Retrieved from http://www.ecowas.int/about-ecowas/history/

AFP. (27 October 2017) Election complaints overshadow Liberia presidential runoff. *Sunday Times: Times Live.* Retrieved from https://www.timeslive.co.za/news/africa/2017-10-27-election-complaints-overshadow-liberia-presidential-runoff/

Lennart Dodoo. (Nov. 23 2017). Liberian Students Rush to CDC For WASSCE Fees As Gov't Withdraws Financial Aid. Retrieved from https://frontpageafricaonline.com/

news/2016news/liberian-students-rush-to-cdc-for-wassce-fees-as-gov-t-withdraws-financial-aid/

The New Dawn. (20 July 2017). Liberia: Ecowas Raises Elections Concerns. *AllAfrica.com.* Retrieved from https://allafrica.com/stories/201707200774.html

New York Times. (Dec. 28 2017). George Weah wins Liberia Election. Retrieved from https://www.nytimes.com/2017/12/28/world/africa/george-weah-liberia-election.html

Reuters. (October 17 2017). Liberia's Johnson Sirleaf rejects accusations of election interference. *Reuters.* Retrieved from https://www.reuters.com/article/us-liberia-election/liberias-johnson-sirleaf-rejects-accusations-of-election-interference-idUSKBN1CZ29D

Prue Clarke, Mae Azango. (Oct. 9 2017). The Tearing Down of Ellen Johnson Sirleaf. *Foreign Policy.* Retrieved from https://foreignpolicy.com/2017/10/09/the-tearing-down-of-ellen-johnson-sirleaf-liberia-elections/

Cholo Brooks. (December 22, 2017). Sen. Taylor Embarrasses Ellen At Gbarnga-Medicoma Road Ground Breaking Ceremony. *Global News Network, Liberia.* Retrieved from http://gnnliberia.com/2017/12/22/senator-jewel-howard-taylor-embarrasses-president-sirleaf-gbarnga-medicoma-road-ground-breaking-ceremony/

Rodney D. Sieh. (2018). Liberia: Pres. Weah 'Copies' Ex-Pres. Sirleaf's Excuse for Failing On Corruption Fight.

Front Page Africa. Retrieved from https://allafrica.com/stories/201808200578.html

TradingEconomies.(2018).LiberiaGDPpercapita:1960-2018. Retrieved from https://tradingeconomics.com/liberia/gdp-per-capita

United Nations Mission in Liberia. (2018). Closure of UNML. Retrieved from https://unmil.unmissions.org/

World Atlas. (2018). President of Liberia through history. Retrieved from https://www.worldatlas.com/articles/presidents-of-liberia-through-history.html

Reuters in Monovia. (14 Jan. 2018). Ellen Johnson Sirleaf, Liberia's outgoing president, expelled by party. *The Guardian.* Retrieved from https://www.theguardian.com/world/2018/jan/14/ellen-johnson-sirleaf-liberia-outgoing-president-expelled-unity-party

Leroy M. Sonpon, III. (January 29, 2018). Pres. Weah Delivers First State of the Nation Address Today. *Daily Observer.* Retrieved from https://www.liberianobserver.com/news/president-weah-delivers-first-state-of-the-nation-address-today/

William Q. Harmon. (March 16, 2018). Weah's LEITI AppointmentSparksCivilSocietyOutrage.*DailyObserver.* Retrieved from https://www.liberianobserver.com/news/weahs-leiti-appointment-sparks-civil-society-outrage/

Edwin G. Genoway, Jr. (15, May, 2018). Liberia: Gurley Gibson Not Rejected-Liberian Government Clarifies

Speculations. *Front Page Africa.* Retrieved from https://allafrica.com/stories/201805210654.html

Koolonline. (May 5 2018). CDC Vicious Purging Continues-As Chairman Morlu Instructs Agencies To Act Accordingly. [Blog] Retrieved from http://www.koolonline2.com/2018/05/05/cdc-vicious-purging-continues-as-chairman-morlu-instructs-agencies-to-act-accordingly/

Wadr. (28, 05, 2018). Liberia: Burkinabé businessman admits giving plane to Weah. Retrieved from http://www.wadr.org/home/index.php?p=highlight&lang=en&auth_=673

Leroy M. Sonpon, III. (June 7, 2018). House to Approve US$957.2m Loans in 72 hours. *Daily Observer.* Retrieved from https://www.liberianobserver.com/news/house-to-approve-two-loans-within-72-hours/

By admin. (Aug 3, 2018). World Bank Rescues Liberia Amid Concern of ETON, EBOMAF Loan Deals Delay. *Front Page Africa.* Retrieved from https://frontpageafricaonline.com/business/economy/world-bank-rescues-liberia-amid-concern-of-eton-ebomaf-loan-deals-delay/

Front Page Africa. (Sept. 3 2018). Liberia: Misguided Weah Must Steer The Shape Of His Presidency. Retrieved from https://frontpageafricaonline.com/editorial/liberia-misguided-weah-must-steer-the-shape-of-his-presidency

News Public Trust. (September 19, 2018). BREAKING NEWS: Gov't invites FBI, IMF, Civil Society on Missing billions inquest panel. *Public Trust Media.* Retrieved from https://newspublictrust.com/2018/09/19/breaking-news-govt-invites-fbi-imf-civil-society-on-missing-billions-inquest-panel/

Lennart Dodoo. (21 September 2018). Liberia: Finance Minister Samuel Tweah Contradicts Previous Admission of Missing Money. *Front Page Africa.* Retrieved from https://allafrica.com/stories/201809210452.html

William Q. Harmon. (September 28, 2018). L$16 Billion Probe Intensifies; 35 CBL Employees Barred from Travel. Retrieved from https://www.liberianobserver.com/news/l16-billion-probe-intensifies-35-cbl-employees-barred-from-travel/

Moses Uneh Yahmia. (October 2, 2018). The March Against "Stolen" 16 billion Liberian Dollars: A Dress Rehearsal to an Imminent and Inevitable Danger. *The Perspective, Atlanta, Georgia*

Admin. (Oct. 3, 2018). EDITORIAL: Liberia's Missing Billions Saga Just Died An Unnatural Death. *Front Page Africa.* Retrieved from https://frontpageafricaonline.com/editorial/editorial-liberias-missing-billions-saga-just-died-an-unnatural-death/

Admin. (Oct 4, 2018). Liberia: US House Committee Passes Resolution To Support Execution of TRC Report. *Front Page Africa.* Retrieved from admin. (Nov 28, 2018). LIBERIA: Gurley Gibson, Previously Nominated

Ambassador to US, Gets UK Posting. *Front Page Africa.* Retrieved from https://frontpageafricaonline.com/ diaspora/liberia-gurley-gibson-previously-nominated-ambassador-to-us-gets-uk-posting/

By admin. (Dec 27, 2018). Liberia: Former Information Minister Wants Eugene Nagbe Expelled from the Press Union of Liberia. *Front Page Africa.* Retrieved from https://frontpageafricaonline.com/politics/liberia-former-information-minister-wants-eugene-nagbe-expelled-from-the-press-union-of-liberia/

Biography.com. (2019). Bob Marley Biography: Songwriter, Singer (1945–1981). *A & Television Network.* Retrieved from https://www.biography.com/people/bob-marley-9399524

Biography.com. (2019). Tyler Perry Biography: Film Actor, Playwright, Screenwriter, Actor, Filmmaker (1969–). *A & E Television Network.* Retrieved from https://www.biography.com/people/tyler-perry-361274

Biography.com. (2019). Aretha Franklin Biography: Singer (1942–2018). *A & E Television Network.* Retrieved from https://www.biography.com/people/aretha-franklin-9301157

Constituteproject.org. (2019). Liberia's Constitution of 1986. Retrieved from https://www.constituteproject.org/ constitution/Liberia_1986.pdf?lang=en

Printed in the United States
By Bookmasters